I0620013

Genesis of a Genre

The Birth of Christian Rock

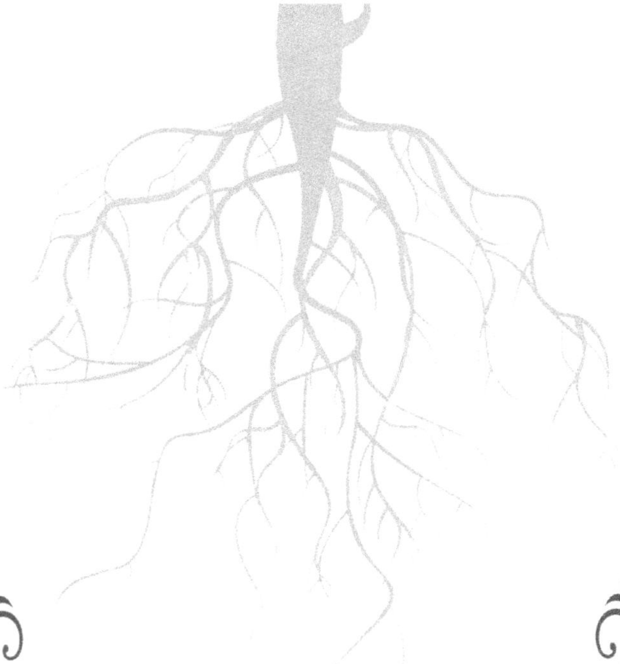

Joe Markko

Copyright 2023 by Joe Markko
All Rights Reserved

ISBN: 979-8-218-23544-4 (paperback)
ISBN: 979-8-218-23545-1 (eBook)
Library of Congress Control Number: 2023912719

Published by Home Before Midnight LLC.
850 Euclid Ave Ste 819 #3107
Cleveland, Ohio 44114 US
team@homebeforemidnight.com

All images are reprinted with permission from:

the Caban Agape Archive, Lesa Caldarella-Wong, Chere [Hess] Vanni, Richard Acevedo, Mike Jungman and Burgess Photographic, Mountain Home Village, California.

Poetry by Lesa Caldarella-Wong from her book, "Desert of this Beauty," reprinted with permission.

Transcriptions for all recorded interviews, The Happy Scribe.com

Except in the case of brief quotations embodied in critical articles or reviews no part of this book may be used or reproduced in any manner whatsoever without written permission from the author.

Disclaimer

This volume should not be confused with a forensic history. It's a story, built upon the faded memories of ex-hippie septuagenarians, none of whom kept notes.

It is conceivable, therefore, that an *actual* historian may discover an occasional bit that proves suspect. I pray that the greater truth of it all will survive the scrutiny of Time.

This is their story as they told it to me.

Ancora Imparo.

Dedication

For the Lost Tribes of Covina Park

"We had a big God.
We had our own song.

We didn't need any convention.

No diamonds.
No gold.

Only silver spoon rings and promises.

Thought it would never end.

But everyone has
to meet themselves –

So we gather our
Altars to begin
again." [1]

---

[1] "Glendora Promises," *Desert of this Beauty*, Lesa Caldarella, Inkwell Books, 2019

Contents

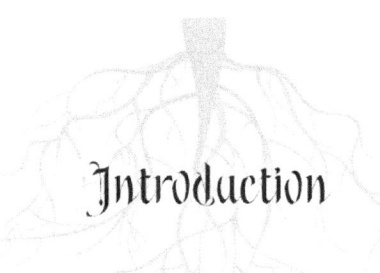

Introduction

Since the days when primitive men first used sticks to beat out messages on hollow logs, every great "Movement" in history has come with its own Soundtrack. "When words fail, music speaks." [Hans Christian Anderson]

In 1910, Joe Hill, the "Troubadour of Discontent," was a well-known martyr and labor folk hero with the *Industrial Workers of the World*. He correctly observed, "You make a speech and people forget about it the next day. You put the information in a leaflet and people hold onto it for a week and throw it away. But if you write a song, and put that information in a song, people hear it, remember it and sing it: it lives on."

The music of the *Suffrage Movement* at the beginning of the 20th Century featured original lyrics that were sung to popular, often patriotic tunes of the day such as "Yankee Doodle" and "When Johnny Comes Marching Home Again." Original music, like Dame Ethel Smyth's famous anthem of the movement, "The March of the Women," served to galvanize those who, in political and religious circles, were denied a voice.

When, in June of 1911, L.A. Police told them that "Votes for Women" speeches were prohibited, the Suffragists set their speeches to music and sang their gospel instead.

Songs of the *American Labor Movement* called for just wages, dignity and a fair shake. They voiced grievances, affirmed the value of the worker to society and expressed hope for life in a more just world. Woody Guthrie, Pete Seeger, Joe Glazer, the Almanac Singers and more, chronicle the history of the American Labor Movement in song.

America's *Civil Rights Movement*, singing a collective "We Shall Overcome," wove Gospel and Jazz into its own, plaintive voice. From Sam Cook singing "A Change is Gonna Come" to Odetta's "Oh, Freedom," the voice of pain expressed itself in more songs than may ever be known.

The *United Farm Worker's Movement*, with César Chávez and Dolores Huerta, offered songs that spoke of the People's heroes, Benito Juárez and Emiliano Zapata. Under their banner of *"¡Si, se puede!"* (Yes, we can!), they spread the word through songs like "El

Picket Sign," "¡*Vivc la Revolución!*" and *"La Peregrinación."* (The Pilgrimage)

In most cases, composers and lyricists are so obscure that we know nothing about them other than their names. They are only remembered because of their connection with the Movement that gave them wings and a song.

Esoteric voices known only by historians, collectors and PBS documentarians, their music helped propel the masses by binding them together under their common banner.

One of the recurring themes of all such crusades was a focus on crucial matters of equity, justice and social reform. Those issues informed their doctrine and rhetoric, spilling over into the lyrical content of their songs. Focused on "speaking truth to power," their intentions were to influence the thinking and behavior of the "Powers That Be."

But the *Jesus Movement*, starting in 1968, was an entirely different kettle of fish. With doctrines of Justification, Regeneration and Reconciliation, the "Jesus People" focused on becoming "salt and light," changing the world around them via Christ within them.

While other movements depended on political and social *pressure* to facilitate change, the Jesus Movement depended on *surrender* to a Divine Plan.

There is argument about whether *the Jesus Movement* was an actual revival or just another cultural ripple that eventually went the way of all religious fads. I make no apology for being convinced that the Jesus Movement was a unique dispensation of God's grace telling the world, "I am still here. I still love you."

It wasn't by accident that it all started in the most populous, and most culturally influential, County in America: Los Angeles.

In 1968, Evangelicals began reaching out to counterculture youth then flooding into Southern California by the tens of thousands. Among these were David Berg's "Teens for Christ" in Huntington Beach, Arthur Blessitt's "His Place" and Don Williams' "Salt Company" coffeehouses, both in Los Angeles.

Carrying the message of the Movement were bands like Sunrise, Joy, Kentucky Faith, New River and Crossroads; Love Song, True Light, Freedom and Children of Light; The Celebration, Kindergarten and Heaven and Earth.

One band who shared the stage with all of them, as well as Larry Norman, Randy Stonehill and Dennis Agajanian, was the Southern California power-trio, Agăpē.

Chronicling the Soundtrack of *the Jesus Movement,* historians recorded the band's relevance to that moment in time.

"The Los Angeles area band, Agape (pronounced uh-GAH-pay) was certainly one of the first Jesus Rock bands, and its story was prototypical of many groups that would spring up in later years all across the country." [*God's Forever Family*, Larry Eskridge]

"The Jesus Movement looked to already existing forms of communication. Alternative Christian newspapers became popular. Dance, drama, mime and other media were used. And, in perhaps the most lasting development, the Jesus movement turned to rock music. Modern Jesus music was invented and artists such as Agape and the All Saved Freak Band burst on the scene." [*The Liturgical Renewal Movement*, John W. Riggs]

"While the Beatles communed with the Maharishi and practiced Transcendental Meditation, radio stations adopted Jesus Rock formats featuring groups such as Love Song, Agape and the All Saved Freak Band." [*American Jesus: How the Son of God Became a National Icon*, Stephen R. Prothero]

"To many churches and religious leaders, the Jesus Movement was a threat. As soon as the first, few bands – the All Saved Freak Band, Agape and Love Song, along with solo artists such as Larry Norman and Randy Stonehill hit the scene, preachers rose up to call them twisted." [*Raised By Wolves: The Story of Christian Rock & Roll*, John J. Thompson and Dinah K. Kotthoff]

Circulating those quotes among former band members, I was curious about whether or not they were aware of them. They were as surprised by the information as I was by the response.

"Do you believe it?" I was asked.

"Believe what?" I responded. "Do I believe what the Jesus Music historians said about Agape?"

"Yeah. Do you believe it? Do you think it's true?"

Moved by the humility and gentle honesty of their questions, I reflected on the idea that band members may have never considered any notion of a legitimate "legacy."

Distracted by the dark clouds that eventually over-shadowed their joy, reminiscing brought too much pain, too much sorrow. So, they simply stopped paying attention.

Agape isn't remembered because they were the best musicians, wrote the best songs or made the biggest splash. They are remembered because *they were there*; because they were verified eyewitnesses to a great Movement; because they carried the banner of the Cross on the frontlines of the battle.

And, also, because they were *very* loud. While other emerging "Jesus Music" bands busied themselves with beautiful melodies and emotionally evocative harmonies, Agape shocked people with their unapologetically raw, Rock 'n Roll edge.

"They played Jesus rock at its crustiest – music which cut through the th ckest defenses of the non-Christian rock fans. For those to whom hard rock music was language, Agape spoke clearly." [*Classic Christian Rockzine*, Fred Edmonson]

In their youth, they gambled on Jesus and "cast their bread upon the waters." Fifty years later, without their knowledge or consent, it was all coming back to them, "good measure, pressed down and running over."

The story of Agape is a story of beginnings: the *Genesis of a Genre* It's a story about the birth of a vision, planted in the "sons and daughters" of Joel's prophecy, that has now influenced three generations for Christ.

It's a tale about "the days of old" and the birth of Christian Rock, when minstrels became messengers and the Word became flesh once again.

Change of Heart

eing 17 and smitten has opened the door to more adventures than youthful imaginations are equipped to handle. Mike Jungman wouldn't be here at all if he hadn't transferred from Gladstone High School pursuing another of those faces that could "launch a thousand ships."

While the romance of teenage fantasies seldom works out, the adventures sometimes do. Of those that do, only a handful leave a lasting legacy, something their fertile minds never saw coming.

It was 1968 and the big news at Azusa High School had to do with students at Garfield High in neighboring East Los Angeles, most of them Mexican Americans, walking out of class to demand better educational opportunities.

The largest mobilization of Chicano youth leaders in American history, the walkouts spread to other campuses including Azusa High School. ("*Insurgency: 1968 Aztec Walkout.*" Victor Gonzalez)

Located about 20 miles Northeast of downtown Los Angeles – and stretching along America's legendary "Mother Road," Route 66 – Azusa, California boasted about 25,000 souls that year. Sitting on the northern end of the San Gabriel Valley placed the city at the foot of the San Gabriel Mountains. Palm trees and mountains. What's not to like?

New to Azusa, Mike's reputation as a drummer was spreading quickly. Playing publicly when he was twelve, with a 6th Grade band called "The Challenger Five," his ambitions quickly blossomed into wanting to be the best drummer in the world. "How does Mitch Mitchell *play* those riffs, anyway?"

Starting his musical journey playing trombone for two years, he had the "misfortune of going to a 'Sock-hop,' where the Safaris played '*Wipe Out.*'"

"Seeing all the girls hanging around the drummer wrecked my trombone career," Mike joked.

Walking across Campus, he was approached by another student.

No warm, friendly greeting of someone welcoming a new person to school, no extended hand, no "Hello, I'm Jeff Newman." Just a straight-to-the-point,

"They tell me you play drums."

"Yeah," Mike responded, "I do."

"I never thought of myself as a good drummer because I was so critical," Mike told me. "But clearly, I'm getting picked up all over the place. People wanted me to play."

Jeff continued, "Well, I play Lead guitar and our band is auditioning drummers." They actually had a drummer at the time. They were lookin' to upgrade.

At their first gig a few months before, *The White Klapp* won the Azusa High School "Battle of the Bands" against groups including "Sound Proof Cookie Jar," "The Nuclear Test Band" and "Flesh and Blood." With such impressive *bona fides*, Mike thought it might be worth a listen.

Showing up for the audition, he set up his Drum-kit next to Jeff's amp.

Dialing in his gear, setting up the sonic-feedback loop that starts the Hendrix song, "Foxy Lady," Jeff didn't recognize, or care about, the look of pain on Mike's face. Recoiling from the intense volume, Mike looked at Jeff and asked, "*Heeey maaaan*, can you turn that down a little?"

Establishing the order of things right off the bat, Jeff snapped, "Look, man, you play drums; I'll play guitar."

"Jeff was a standout player," Mike mentioned.

"Exacting, ala Don Felder. He wasn't interested in much else. Rehearsals we're mostly about getting *his* parts down."

Those kinds of issues tend to rub the rest of the band the wrong way. But Jeff marched to his own cadence; it didn't matter if you liked it or not.

He started playing near the beginning of his freshman year. "I just grabbed the guitar and, playing like someone who was learning to play third base, I just kept doing it over, and over, and over again."

With Fred Caban on Bass, Major Cornell on Organ and Billy Avalos with Vocals, The White Klapp took off with a sonic roar.

Setting their collective volumes on "11," and selecting the Iron Butterfly classic, "In a Gadda Da Vida" for the audition, they shook the foundations of the garage. Mike later observed, "I nailed it man. At least I must have, because I got the gig."

Fred Caban was also a transfer to Azusa from Roosevelt High School in East L.A. He was another Lead Guitarist of note, playing bass with the group only because Jeff wasn't going to give that up for anybody. "I made more money playing bass than I ever did playing guitar," Fred later told Larry Eskridge for his opus, *"God's Forever People: The Jesus People Movement in America."*

Learning his first guitar chords, G and E Minor, at age seven, from a house painter his father hired, Fred took off and "figured out how to play." At age twelve, while Mike was jammin' across town, Fred was playing professionally with several James Brown-style funk bands in East L. A.

After a few months of playing "covers," the Klapp was convinced that they were ready to be stars in the California "scene." Though they'd played only a few, simple gigs, they felt they had conquered Azusa and spread their vision to the larger world. Calculating that the only thing they lacked was funding, they hatched a teen-age plan.

"We wanted to have a hit record and be famous so we were out trying to find our future," Fred commented. "We knew some people in San Juan Capistrano who were artists and painters who had money. We were trying to contact them to see if they would be interested in helping us out, sort of funding it all. "

The only problem was that Billy wanted Jeff to go along and Fred wasn't into it. Jeff was Eric Clapton. Fred was Jimmie Hendrix. Both musicians played a form of Blues-based Rock but they were worlds apart, both in their musical sensibilities and the sounds they each wanted to pursue.

Jeff's comment on the tensions between them was pretty simple: "Fred was playing lead on bass, basically, but that's fine." He could tolerate that much.

Billy talked Fred into taking Jeff. It was his car, after all. Prepared to spend the night on the beach, somewhere, the three of them jammed sleeping bags and guitars into Billy's VW "bug" and headed south on the Pacific Coast Highway.

The trip to San Juan ended up being nothing more than a waste of time, so they arbitrarily decided to divert to Huntington Beach, "Surf City USA."

"We were in the general area, anyway," Fred mentioned. Serendipity.

The ocean waves at Huntington are different than anywhere else along the Pacific Coast. Enhanced by the manner in which the open-ocean swells around Catalina Island, there is consistent surf, year-round.

With an average 3 to 4-foot wave every 16 seconds, and an average water temperature of 72 degrees, Huntington Beach has always been a Westcoast surfing mecca.

They were young teens fresh out of High School, the Rock gods seemed to be smiling on them, and the Beach was calling. Why not? For budding rock stars with a deflated plan, it was a pleasant consolation prize on such a gorgeous, Southern California day.

Jeff commented, "We had last eaten the day before, at a Taco Bell, and I remember getting a Taco burrito. For us, just eating was a big deal because we didn't have any money. We're all broke, sleeping on the Beach, trying to make sure we don't get run over."

Next morning, walking along the Pacific shore, they were approached by a few people working out of a storefront at the end of Main Street known as "The Jesus Light Club."

Operated by a group calling themselves, "Teens for Christ," they had clearly capitalized on the credentials of the building's previous tenants, the "Gospel Light Club" run by Dave Wilkerson's *Teen Challenge*. No sense letting a good reputation go to waste.

"You guys hungry?" they asked.

Seriously? The trio quickly grabbed the concept.

"*Sooooo*, if you go and listen to something about Jesus, they give you a sandwich," Jeff laughed. "Well, yeah, we'll go for that."

Leaving the Beach, walking across the Highway, entering Main Street, their hosts yelled at everyone they encountered to "Get right with God." This was going to be different.

Fred observed, "They prayed for the food; then we sat down to eat. After we ate, I noticed they closed and locked the door. They gave us each the Gospel of John and started praying.

And then we realized what we had gotten into. This was some kind of religious group and they caught us.

But I'd never seen young people so in love with Christ, so in love with God. It was just something unusual. I mean, I'd seen Krishnas and others from the Eastern religions that were common in those days, but this was the first time I'd ever seen Christians that were actually bonkers for Jesus. There were, maybe, 20-25 people there."

Jeff offered, "I'm in this place with Freddie and Billy and they started going around the room asking people, 'What do you think about Jesus? Or what do you think about God? Or what do you think about spiritual things?'

I'd never heard Freddie or Billy ever talk about God. And so, we all start sharing what we thought. Fred had his metaphysical stuff, which is weird, but that's Fred. Billy and I were Catholic so we're pulling out our Catholic catechism stuff. We're just laying it out there, listening to each other and ourselves.

Then, all of a sudden, there's this guy named Michael and he asks, 'Can I share with you what I think about God?' And when he started talking, God showed us the Holy Spirit. The whole room changed. I was dumb-founded. And he wasn't saying anything profound but what he did say was empowered by the Holy Spirit. And God's Spirit was just drilling into our hearts."

Michael was a recent convert, part of David Berg's *Family International,* established earlier that year. One year *after* their meeting, David Berg and his congregation of 50-75 teens would abandon Huntington Beach. Running from Police pressures, they took to the road in buses.

While camping in Louis and Clark Park, a local news reporter first called them, "The Children of God." Noting that every great Movement will spawn fringe-groups, popping up along its shadowed edges, the COG became one of the most destructive, pseudo-Christian cults to come out of the Jesus Movement.

But whatever they became in the future, on that night, Michael and his friends shed light on the paths of "the San Gabriel Boys." On that night, God's Word, in the mouths of strangers, was guidance for Fred Caban, Jeff Newman and Billy Avalos.

"When we were asked if we wanted to accept Christ as Lord and Savior, I had one question," Jeff stated.

"I love the guitar. What's going to happen now that I'm following Jesus? Do I have to give up my music?

And Michael said, 'You can use it for Jesus.' And that was the answer I wanted to hear."

They bowed their heads and, as much as their teenage brains were capable of understanding, they accepted Christ as their Savior.

"Going back to the Beach that night, everything's changed," Jeff told me. "The veil that was over my eyes had been lifted. I'm looking at everything differently. I'm looking at reality through different eyes. I'm looking at the sand, sleeping on the Beach and I'm just freaking out."

As for Fred, he had a conversation with the Almighty. "'If you're out there, reveal yourself to me. Were those people speaking truth?' And then I had a true encounter, a spiritual encounter, where I felt like Jesus physically came to me on the Beach, put His hand on me and told me to follow Him."

Speaking of the instant *Change of Heart,* Fred observed, "I think a lot of people don't understand why the Beach was so important for us.

Jeff and I were rivals. We were contemporaries and friends, but when it came to playing guitar, he always ended up playing the leads I wanted to play. There were times when we hated each other's guts.

But when we got back to the Beach and hugged each other, it was a hug of forgiveness. I forgot the guy didn't like me. We're brothers now in Christ. We didn't verbalize it but that's what it was."

In that embrace, Fred Caban and Jeff Newman
suddenly found themselves somewhere they'd never
been: a place where God's presence is so real that
yesterday and tomorrow no longer matter; when
forever becomes the new frame of reference.

In a single heartbeat of time, they became keenly
aware that they were already "ankle-deep" in the
Stream of Eternity.

Purposing to move in the rhythm of its flow, a "Great
Depth" was now alive within them. Old things had
passed away. All things were becoming new.

The White Klapp, and all of its youthful delusions, was
dead. A burial at Sea would take place shortly.

Awakening early, and hoping they might get a bite to
eat before heading home, the trio took a few minutes
to walk back to the Jesus Light Club.

Spotted walking in, they were greeted, "Oh, hey,
you're here, man. We're going to have a party, okay?
A Baptism Party!"

Procuring their arsenal as they readied themselves,
the "Teens for Christ" brandished their well-worn
signs declaring "Jesus is the Way, Turn to God, Repent
and Jesus is Lord."

Raggedy, rowdy and one elephant shy of a Circus
Parade, two dozen hippies bum-rushed the door,

spilled onto Main Street and celebrated every joy-filled step to the ocean.

Jeff continued the story. "And we're like, in the middle of this group of Jesus people and they're just obnoxious evangelicals. They were shouting at people as we walked, about how they needed to get right. Watching all of this I'm thinking, *is this what I'm supposed to do*? It's my first impression.

So, we crossed the Pacific Coast Highway; it probably took us less than a couple of minutes. We were approaching the Pier and, all of a sudden, a loud voice mocked the signs: *'Buddha is Lord.'*"

The iconic City pier at Huntington Beach is one of the longest piers on the West Coast. Jutting 1,850 feet into the Pacific Ocean, the deck is 30 feet above sea level. Used during the Second World War as a spotting station for enemy submarines, it was the center of the City's prominent beach culture.

With detractors shouting from the top of the Pier, "It was like throwing a rock into a pack of dogs." Jeff commented. "What do you think happened? Everyone is carrying on and I'm thinking, Dang, this is bizarre. This is warfare, right? There's warfare here. There's something going on.

So, we walked into the Pacific, just off the Pier, and they dunk us.

We're dripping wet, drying ourselves off with the towels we brought. But we have nothing to change into. We were wearing what we left home in two days before. They stuffed our pockets full of tracts, we headed back to Azusa and *we were out of our minds*."

Maybe. Maybe it was just that; a temporary loss of reality brought on by the prolonged use of psychedelic drugs combined with an intense, emotional experience. Fifty years of accumulated evidence suggests that would be an incorrect diagnosis.

Their experience, and those of the other pilgrims they would encounter along the way, pointed clearly to the fiery passion of youth embracing the Divine. Like the disciples on the Road to Emmaus, their entire being had been enflamed: "Did not our hearts *burn* within us?" Though they were young, they had never been more lucid.

Whatever critics or nay-sayers may conjecture; whatever Psychologists or Theorists may surmise, this much is certain: *something happened!* Something wonderful, something forever. They couldn't fully explain it, then or now, but their lives had just changed, irrevocably.

Three seventeen-year-old boys, now full of wonder, were taking their first, feeble steps on a journey that would ultimately draw thousands of people to the banner of God's unyielding love.

Walt Whitman wrote, "Our rendezvous is fitly appointed. God will be there and wait 'til we come." [1]

Fred, Jeff and Billy left home in search of Patrons for their art, in search of a Door to Fame. They had no idea that God was waiting for them in a small, storefront building at the end of Main Street. That sounds like something Rod Serling might say in the opening monologue of a *"Twilight Zone"* episode, but it is the uncontested fact of their shared history.

If Fred had not transferred schools; if he had prevailed and Jeff didn't come along; if they had not diverted to Huntington Beach; if they had not been out of money and very hungry, they would have missed their appointment.

Following the next, natural option each step of the way, they stumbled through *the Unsought Door*, now blown open by the gentle breath of God.

"I was found of them that sought me not; I was made manifest unto them that asked not after me." [2]

---

[1] Walt Whitman, "Leaves of Grass." 1855
[2] Isaiah 65:1

Believe

verwhelmed by the avalanche of "mind-blowing" stimuli, the trip home was more introspective than celebratory, more, "what are we really getting into?" than anything resembling the giggling remnant of a Hippie "Baptism Party."

"It was very quiet." Fred remembered. "Like, this was *way* above our pay grade. Now what do we do? How do we handle this? Do we keep in the Bible? Do we keep playing?"

Pulling out their new copies of the Gospel of John, Jeff and Fred started reading at the first verse, each occasionally reading aloud something they discovered as, "very cool."

At this point, the only thing they knew for sure was, they were supposed to preach. That's what they learned at the Beach. "If you're really saved, you'll tell somebody about it. Might as well tell everybody."

Following the 30-minute drive from Huntington Beach, Jeff asked Billy to drop him off at home where his mom was just starting her day.

"It's early in the morning; I get into the house and call to my mom, "Mom, I got saved! *I got saved!*"

Jocelyn was a single mother raising five children on her own. Working in the School Cafeteria all those years, she'd seen enough teenagers "under the influence" to spot a stoner in a quick hurry. She also knew her boy.

"Can you come in the room, son?" she asked. "And turn on the light."

Jeff knew she was "staring hard" at his eyes. "She knows that I'm stoned all the time," he said.

"And she sees how lucid I am and starts to cry realizing, 'Oh, my God, you *are* saved.' And eventually I start leading all of my family to the Lord."

Meanwhile, Fred went somewhere he was pretty sure he'd find some of his old friends. The gentle impulse of newly found joy, the "overflow of the cup," was now driving him and, like Jeff, he had to "tell somebody."

Jay Orr was another local drummer whose parents had a second building on the back of their property. It became a practice space, hang-out and crash-pad for several other bands in the area. After testifying to whoever was there. Fred sat down, picked up the phone and started calling everyone else he knew.

While Fred was burnin' up Jay's phone and Jeff was talking to his mom, Mike Jungman was sitting in Major Cornell's back yard getting high.

Major asked, "Did you talk to Jeff?"

"No," Mike croaked between puffs, "Why?"

"Well, they're preaching up at the House."

"So, we finished getting loaded and went up there. Their clothes were still damp from being baptized and they are *LIT UP*," Mike emphasized.

Continuing his narrative, he said, "Something crazy happened to them. I kind of said, 'Wow! What did they take?' Within a few days, Fred's at my house asking me if I want to pray, to ask Jesus into my heart. And my first thought was, 'Jesus is a good guy, who doesn't like Jesus, right?'

I just knew I wanted *something* in my life, so I prayed. No fireworks like they had which, of course, was my gauge until the next day."

Hitchhiking home, the day after praying with Fred, Mike jumped into a car with four guys smokin' herb.

"They hand me the joint and I passed it up without saying much more than, 'No thanks.' Getting out of the car I turned toward home thinking, *'No thanks?'*

I'd been high every day since I was 14, I'm not exaggerating, on whatever was available. The music didn't work without drugs. The girlfriends didn't work without drugs. I mean, all the time. And now out of nowhere, I don't want to get high any more.

And there was no emotion attached to it, to the whole repenting, conversion thing. God had touched my heart without me knowing it; no fireworks, no cracks in the ceiling. And since that day, I've never been tempted. Drugs were gone."

The power of it all is that they weren't experiencing this revolution in a vacuum. Unknown to them was the fact that, all over southern California, people just like them were having experiences just like theirs. People were changing, suddenly, drastically and for the better.

The seeds of the coming Movement now seemed scattered on the wind. Organic, spontaneous and disconnected from organized religion, a change was coming to Christianity in America.

Though the previous day's prayer with Fred opened the door for Mike, it was the dramatic, seismic shift in Jeff that convinced him that the whole "Jesus thing" was for real.

"Fred, you could explain away. He was always philosophical, into this kind of stuff all the time. But

Jeff was, I'm trying to think, I can't think of a better word, ... just narcissistic.

I remember him throwing his mum out of the house so we could rehearse once, okay? Jeff was this intense guy that, all of a sudden, truly cared about me. The change in him was so striking to me."

The friends had been rock 'n roll buddies long enough to see each other at their worst. They'd all been witness to the terrible choices and unguarded impulses that often seem to accompany youthful indulgence.

But now, they were each profoundly different, and everyone who knew them could see it. There was no subterfuge, no pretense, no regret.

While "Billy Lee" Avalos shared the same experience as Fred and Jeff, his journey would take him in an entirely different direction.

"I don't know what happened to him," Fred stated. "It was the strangest thing, but he disappeared. He was there and then he wasn't."

That's because Billy decided to go back to school and enlist in the Military. Stationed with the 1st Armored Division in Germany during the Vietnam Era, he returned home and worked at the City of Hope Medical Center for 24 years.

Married in 1987, he raised two children and passed away in February, 2011 after a lengthy battle with Cancer.

His Obituary read, in part, "He was a man who took pride in upholding his beliefs; his faith was important to him. He became a Christian as a young adult. He was a good man. *He won the Battle of the Bands.*" [1]

Amazing, the stories we choose to pass down.

Unlike his compadres, Billy had no interest in any notion of "ministry." Like the majority of Believers, he lived a life of gentle influence, touching lives for Christ along the way.

Spending a month or so traveling between Azusa and Huntington, Mike, Fred, Jeff and a dozen of their friends were radicalized with a lethal dose of evangelistic fervor.

Planning events that would now be known as "Pop up Crowds," they and their friends from *Teens for Christ* invaded every shopping mall in the area with the full fury of a summer storm. They came; they saw; they conquered.

Mike mentioned, "We're just out in the streets, Fred and I in particular, so you couldn't get down the street without getting hit with the Gospel. And it wasn't

---

[1] dignitymemorial.com/obituaries/glendora-ca/william-avalos-4575594

because we were great at it. We rarely knew what we were talking about but the experience was so strong and we were so in love with what was going on."

But an inevitable problem, one that would trouble and hurt them for many years, started to show itself: they weren't going to be accepted by the Christian community.

"Based on what we saw from *Teens for Christ*," Mike observed, "we just honestly didn't believe there were any other Christians in the area."

The examples to which they had access were suspect.

Eating at a local restaurant, Mike saw a family praying before they ate. Thinking, "Wow! There's other Christians around," he got up, approached their table and said, "How cool is it that you're praying with your family?!

And the guy looks up at me and says, 'Why don't you cut your hair?'"

Their first experience at being wounded in the House of their Friends, they had no way of knowing that Christians wounding Christians is so common that it's become accepted as a Rite of Passage. They would get over it.

Birthed into the Kingdom as unconventional evangelists, their aggressive approach and bohemian appearance now began to put them at odds with typical, rank-and-file Believers. "We weren't scalpels or fine surgical instruments," they observed, "We were a blunt object."

Jeff added, "People didn't always like to see us coming. We either made you glad, or mad."

Believe! That was the living core of their message. Everything was wrapped up in that.

They weren't Christian apologists, Theologians or Sunday School teachers. They were a voice crying in the wilderness: "Believe in the Lord Jesus Christ and you will be saved." That's all they cared about. It's what drove them.

Indeed, one of the primary, identifying characteristics of the coming Jesus Movement was an unrelenting call to personal evangelism. It sustained them, individually and collectively.

Deciding to witness to people at Citrus College, a local Community College, the new converts took a short-cut through the campus of Azusa Pacific College, directly across the street. "We were going there to tell them what Jesus did in our lives."

Azusa Pacific College (APC), was the first Bible college on the West Coast geared toward preparing men and women for ministry and service. Launched in 1899 by a small group of Quakers and a Methodist evangelist, *the Training School for Christian Workers* embraced the motto of "God First."

Their Alumni includes well known Evangelical voices like Jack W. Hayford, John MacArthur and John Wimber. Eventually becoming the largest employer in Azusa, it was "Kingdom Central" for a lot of people.

Engaging anyone they saw as they crossed the APC Campus, the group was observed by Ray Salmon, a student from the school, who questioned them, "What are you guys doing?"

Explaining their mission, he invited them to a Bible Study in one of the College dorm rooms and began teaching them the Scriptures. Ray was also a part of *Campus Crusade for Christ* and invited them to visit his Church.

Through Ray, they met Russ Chambers and Charlie Eisenberg, a couple of his friends from the Bethany Baptist Church in neighboring West Covina. "They couldn't help but fall in love with us," Mike commented, "so they took us in, taught us the Word of God, and led us to understand *Him* better."

Of course, they fell in love with them. They were very bright spots in an otherwise, very dull Christian arena. By 1968, the great majority of Mainline churches had become stagnant and myopic and were in the process of withering on the Vine. Any anguish for lost souls seemed long buried under a suffocating blanket of propriety.

But every one of those churches also had folks like Russ and Charlie who had long prayed for revival. Delighted for what they saw as an answer to prayer, they embraced the new converts as their personal charges. For them, it was Christmas morning.

Working with Russ and Charley, the group of friends began an invasion of the *Bob's Big Boy* restaurant in West Covina.

The parking lot was often filled with 300-400 people getting high, hanging out, "pickin' up chicks" or just "doin' their thing." Pulling into the lot in the back of a pickup truck, our heroes stood and loudly proclaimed the good news of the Gospel. At least, what they knew of it. Or thought they knew.

They'd been saved only a few months, the proverbial "Babes in Christ." Long on zeal, short on knowledge and wisdom, the growing group hadn't yet learned much about the Christian Faith. But they were convinced of three things:

1) Jesus is real, 2) He's in the business of wiping slates clean and 3) He's coming back to "gather His own."

That last piece of information provided the sense of urgency that's always been the driving force of evangelism. "Jesus is coming! *Any minute now!*"

Sharing those sensibilities, the previously male-dominated group was now well represented by dozens of "liberated" young women. With ardent "Women's Libbers" in the front row of every crowd, the presence of reasoning females among the barbarians somehow made the men more credible to the demonstrative gatherings.

Working shoulder-to-shoulder in the streets, the group of friends went to a local Drive-in Theater and started sharing the Good News on the gravel stretch in front of the Concession Stand.

"I can't tell you how it started," Mike shared, "I can't remember. What I can tell you is that about 50 people ended up kneeling in the gravel and accepting Christ on the spot."

"Boom!" he emphasized. "You could see the Holy Spirit flow over people. And, by the way, I had no idea what those words meant at the time. We didn't have any training."

Overwhelmed by the results, they started thinking, "Now we know what to do." Attempting to duplicate that harvest, they returned to the drive-in every night for the next two weeks.

"We were leading people to the Lord right and left," Jeff Newman added. "And it was so easy. That's what was amazing, man. It seemed that all we had to do was sneeze and people got saved. It was a sovereign thing that God was doing."

"We had no organization, no leaders, and we're learning the Bible where we could. We rarely knew what we were talking about but we were in love with it all," Mike stated.

After watching a Billy Graham Crusade on television, Jeff "got stoked up" and went back to Azusa High School to pass out tracts and witness. The Police chased him away but he returned the next day.

Observing Jeff as he passed out Gospel tracts, the Officer arrested him and took him to the Police Station, charging him with a misdemeanor: Loitering.

An amazing wrinkle in Jeff's story is the fact that he was dating a young lady named Carol Chick, daughter of a man named Jack Chick.

Living in Alhambra, a neighboring community in the San Gabriel Valley, Jack was converted while listening to a radio episode of "The Old-Fashioned Revival Hour" with Charles E. Fuller. When Fuller said, *"Though your sins be as scarlet, they shall be as white as snow,"*[2] Jack knelt and received Christ.

An American graphic novelist, he devoted his art to evangelism. "Chick Tracts" are small, pocket-sized

---

[2] Isaiah 1:18

Gospel tracts with Christian conversion as their message. Over the years, more than 750 million copies of his booklets have been translated into more than 100 languages, making him one of the most widely sold graphic artists in the world.

The fact that his daughter was dating a hippie, Jeff Newman, and hanging out with his heathen friends, rubbed Jack the wrong way.

In his Biography, Jack is quoted as saying, "At the time, I didn't like teenagers or their rebellion. But, all of a sudden, the power of God hit me and my heart broke and I was overcome with the realization that these teens were probably on their way to hell." [3]

Asked by his daughter Carol, Jack, and one of his close friends, accompanied Jeff's mother to the Police Station to "identify my son," she said.

Jeff's mom reminisced with him, "They were very interested in you because you were the leader and everyone seemed to know you. You were like an electrical charge at Azusa High School. You could gather all those high school kids. They were very interested in what God was doing with the youth. "

"So, I'm being put in jail for the Faith," Jeff said, tongue-in-cheek. "No, that's not it, at all. I was being a rebel, exactly what the cop said. So, Jack came and

---

[3] The Biography of Jack Chick, *Chick Publications*, 2016

got me out of jail and eventually stood with me when I went through the court case. They dismissed it."

Spiritually charged and biblically ignorant, the Azusa teenagers now stand in desperate need of some old-fashioned discipling. If they were to endure, if the flame was to continue burning, they would have to feed it with something other than guess-work.

Mike said, "We didn't go to Church. We didn't look for any because we didn't know to do that. God just said, 'Go do that,' and we did it. 'Go do this,' and we did it. We were like Sheep without a Shepherd."

"Wake up. Study the Word. Preach the Word. Rest and Repeat" became their daily blueprint. But they had no idea about the meaning behind most of the things that now thrilled their souls. Unaware of how to apply the wealth of truths they were discovering daily, they quickly came to an end of themselves.

Meanwhile, the gritty, socially tumultuous year of 1968 was also coming to an end. Icons had been assassinated, centers of learning and government were burned, the masses marched, the "heathen raged" and the Police busted heads from Coast to Coast. America was not bettered by any of it.

At the close of 1968, the terms "Jesus People" and "Jesus Movement" were still one year away from being popularized when Duane Pederson launched the *Hollywood Free Paper*.

Larry Norman had just walked away from the group, People!, adopting Hollywood Boulevard as his own mission field. Starting a halfway house for new converts, he spent the royalties earned from Capitol Records buying them clothes and food.

His first album, *Upon This Rock,* was still one year away and the term, "Contemporary Christian Music" was five years away from being "a thing."

At "His Place" on Sunset Strip, the Lead guitarist for the L.A. based, *Pacific, Gas and Electric* found Christ as his Savior. The former guitarist for the Ohio-based, *James Gang*, Glenn Schwartz never toured in support of PG&E's national hit, *"Are you Ready?"*

Returning home instead, Glenn joined forces with two "Gospel Rock" songwriters whose original music was already being featured on their own Saturday night radio program: *"Time for the Risen Christ."* [4]

Though coincidental to the Jesus Movement, the Ohio group was not coincidental to *the Birth of Christian Rock*. The trio would form the nucleus for the *All Saved Freak Band*.

Back at Jesus Movement Central, Pastor Chuck Smith's Calvary Chapel in Costa Mesa brought Lonnie Frisbee

---

[4] "When Someday Comes: Memoirs of a Survivor," Joe Markko, 2011.

on board to work with John Nicholson and John Higgins in "The House of Miracles" outreach.

Reporting 35 converts in the first week, they now number more than 1,000 congregations world-wide.

Don Williams, a young assistant pastor at the Hollywood Presbyterian Church, started talking to the hippies moving into Hollywood. Providing them with a space where they could hear the new Christian rock music, he started the *Salt Company Coffeehouse* in August of that year.

From Santa Barbara down to San Diego, from Long Beach out to Riverside and San Bernadino, something powerful was brewing.

Standing on the first ripples of a coming spiritual and cultural tsunami, the geographically scattered pioneers were seized with a uniformly giddy sense of expectation.

"We woke up excited every morning to see what God was going to do," Mike Jungman reported.

For the deeply entrenched Christian Church in America, the end of 1968 was a moment of schism and new beginnings. Not only for a growing and dynamic mass of youthful pioneers but, ultimately, for the sound of Worship in Churches all over the world.

For now, there was work to be done, an adventure to be lived, miracles to be wrought and personal kingdoms to be torn down. For Fred, Jeff, Mike and Major, the number one love of their lives, music, was temporarily set aside. It would find its own way, for each of them, next year.

But now, they needed a foundation. They needed someone smarter than they imagined themselves to be, someone to help connect the dots. It would take a different kind of person to connect with this growing entourage of zealous, idealistic and self-proclaimed "freaks." Really different.

Funny how things work out. As it happened, Jack Chick had already introduced them to someone special, someone who could guide them on the next step of their journey. He was the unnamed friend Jack brought to the Azusa Police Station to serve as reinforcements for the Liberation of Jeff Newman.

Of all the good people who might have been willing to fill the bill, to rise to the challenge, who better to teach *babes in the Woods,* than "Tarzan and Jane?"

It was time to make sense of it all.

It was time for the birth of dreams in the Garden of Glendora.

The Garden of Dreams

en years before our story begins, Walt Disney was in Switzerland filming the coming-of-age movie, *"Third Man on the Mountain."* When Walt saw the Matterhorn for the first time, he immediately sent a Post Card to his production team, his "Imagineers," w th two words on the back: "BUILD THIS!"

One of the professionals hired for the project was a 57-year-old Chemical Engineer from DuPont named Delbert Wilhite.

Del was part of the team that created the formula for concrete that coulc be sprayed on a form and molded or sculpted into "Artificial Rock." Turning 500 tons of steel and concrete nto Disneyland's "Matterhorn Bobsled Attraction' inspired Del to use the technology for his own dream.

Described variously as a "Storyteller, lovable cartoon character and Priest after the order of Melchizedek," the best snapshot was offered by Major Cornell.

"Del was a scientist who found Jesus on top of an ancient, stone pyramid in Mexico."

He was also Jack Chick's friend.

Del and his wife, "Mother Mary," lived 45 minutes from Disneyland in Glendora. The shared dream of their entire lives was to turn their home into a hospice-care facility for terminally ill children.

Spending years as a Missionary in the rural, mountainous areas of Mexico, Del studied orchids and Tropical birds along the way. Marrying all of that knowledge to the experiences gained at Disney, he built a sanctuary of stone walls, waterfalls and lava flows. He then filled it with exotic birds and a lush Tropical Garden populated with art and curiosities collected in his travels.

Entire walls of the house were windows, like giant television screens looking out on the panorama. Round lights of varied sizes, flush with the ceiling, reminiscent of the "Starship Enterprise," were randomly placed to create the look of a river of stars flowing above you.

His incredibly lush, jungle oasis was so well known that a local magazine, the *Glendoran*, ran a photo-filled article about the Wilhites titled, "Tarzan and Jane." By the beginning of 1969, their home had become a drive-by Tourist attraction.

Taking years to complete, their monumental labor of love would indeed have been a joy-filled Wonderland for dying children. Would have been.

Whatever cruel turn of the cards dashed that dream may never be known, but what we do know is that God had something waiting for them, something equally fulfilling: caring for broken children of another sort.

Had it been scripted by Hollywood, the newly converted, intense y creative and in-a-hurry "psychodeeliacs" couldn't have landed in a better spot.

Nice job, Jack.

Friday night Bible studies at Del and Mary's saw the house overflowing with hippies. Occupying every bit of available space, they sat cross-legged on the floors, open Bibles on their laps.

With large bird cages, Tillandsia and air orchids lining the walls, it was a Friday night paradise for hungry minds, searching souls and stoned hippies. In what must have resemb ed the Casting Call for the movie, *Alice's Restaurant*, there was enough hair in the room to weave a small rug, enough faded blue denim to fashion a large sail.

"Denim so soft it folded into our lives
becoming banner and flag;
patchouli incense wafted
veils over innocence.

Everyone was beautiful
Love and meditation were forever."[1]

Fred began to describe it. "In his living room, he had this huge aviary. It went all the way around the whole living room with orchids, very special orchids from the jungle that he got himself, collected them from Brazil.

And they had all these birds that were very rare birds that lived in there. And this was his living room, where he taught from.

And he'd be standing up or sitting down in the corner. We'd all be huddled there hearing him talk about Armageddon, the last days and prophecies."

Jeff added, "We would come to Del's place and be mesmerized. Oh, my God! And when he started talking about 'Jesus is coming,' I'm serious, we'd walk around with our heads looking up in the sky. *'He's coming any minute.'"*

"It looked like Disneyland, man." Mike said. "All of the fake rock and mountains and stuff like that, all of that,

---

[1] "Curls and Grace," *Desert of This Beauty.* With permission from Lesa Caldarella-Wong

44

that's what he did. The inside of his house and the outside of the house looked like lava pouring out.

And he had these gestures. He would hold his big, nubby-looking finger straight up and then make this gesture of coming through your heart. 'In you and through you,' is the way he would talk about the Holy Spirit working in us."

Mike continued. "And, you know, we're all just in awe. He used to say he was a big zero with the ring rubbed out. God used him in an amazing way. He made us feel like we were the center of the universe."

Working in the street with the two Deacons from Bethany Baptist, attending Bible studies with Del and continuing to meet with Ray in the APC Dorm, the minds of the fellow musicians began to find their focus.

Following his conversion, Fred instinctively knew that a Rock 'n Roll lifestyle was incongruous with his new faith so he laid down his guitar. Trying hard to get his priorities straight, it was the only solution he could think of. "I put down the guitar and told God I wasn't going to play anymore until He told me to pick it up."

"I had pretty much given everything up, music, everything. I just ate, breathed, talked and walked Jesus. Nothing else existed but Jesus. And that was it. I just gave everything up."

True but, from the time Fred heard Michael tell Jeff Newman that he could use his music for the Lord, he'd been thinking about it.

Some people play musical instruments. Others are musicians. Unless granted some kind of special dispensation, true musicians are driven to connect with the sound made by their instruments. It's inevitable. For all similarly possessed people, music isn't a passing fling but a love affair that never ends. It's part of their DNA.

After about three months, Fred began to feel a peace about playing again and started jamming in his garage. Asked about what he played he said, "Oh, I don't know. Anything loud."

Asking Mike if he wanted to jam again, the two friends thought to pick up where they left off: the same, only different. But there was a problem.

"When God opened those doors," Mike stated, "I didn't know where my drums were. No matter what anybody tells you, marijuana affects your memory, okay?"

Whether Jeff had a better memory, or had simply logged more hours flying level through the haze, he remembered, made a call and Mike's Drum kit showed up within a few days. They were in the garage of Phillip Lopez, another local guitarist and friend with whom he'd left them.

Deeming it a small miracle, the rescue of his drums caused Mike to fee like God was opening doors. It emboldened him. "What would you think about using our musical gifts for Jesus?" Mike asked Fred at their next jam session.

Fred smiled. While Mike may have been the first to give it a voice, they were both possessed by the same idea; they'd both been thinking the same thing. Fred and Mike were the core. They would always be the core. As long as they were heart to heart, there would always be a future for their music.

Soon to become a full-fledged vision, another dream was being born in Glendora.

They didn't know how they were going to do it, what they were going to call it or what the results might be. There were no markets, sales categories, radio stations, record stores or audiences that would embrace what they were thinking about doing.

"Will the Church accept it?" was a question they never asked themselves, didn't even think about it. With only one clue, "Let's tell people about Jesus," their minds were made up to try something they would never before have imagined.

At this point, there was no such thing as Christian Rock music. The most progressive of worshippers could, maybe, tolerate a folksy sounding acoustic guitar behind a stellar voice but, Christian Rock? Even

Elvis, the "King of Rock," closed out his performances with an old-timey Gospel song.

The very idea of mingling the "Pure Faith" with music of the Ungodly was anathema to Christians, seeing it as a cheap bastardization of the Gospel and a danger to their youth.

At the end of the 1950s, Dr. Martin Luther King Jr. captured the feelings of the average Believer when it came to the issue. Though he may have later changed his mind about Christian rock, what he wrote in his church's newsletter, *"Advice for Living,"* reveals an accurate reflection of Christian thinking at the time.

"It seems to me that one must decide to either play gospel music or rock and roll. The two are totally incompatible. The profound sacred and spiritual meaning of the great music of the Church must never be mixed with the transitory quality of rock and roll music.

The former serves to lift men's souls to higher levels of reality, and therefore to God; the latter so often plunges men's minds into degrading and immoral depths. *Never seek to mix the two."*

This, generally-held, Christian opinion exempted Gospel powerhouses like the Mighty Clouds of Joy, the Staple Singers, the Five Blind Boys of Alabama and even Sister Rosetta Tharpe, all of whom laid down a groove so sophisticated it had people dancing in the aisles for sheer joy.

If such resistance was the starting point, if that was the cross-wind they would have to fight, it would take an amazing amount of conviction, grit and youthful ignorance to even start down the road.

That's why revival always begins with the young or the poor: they haven't yet learned what they cannot do.

The first need, a bass player. Like everything else so far, the pieces were already in place. Like everything else, it was the next, natural step.

"If the answer is simple, God is speaking." [Einstein]

Lanore "Lonnie" Campbell was well known among musicians in the area. "She played flute, trombone, double bass, basscon and all kinds of stuff," Mike pointed out. "All the Glendora musicians knew Lonnie, so, for her to play was great. And we figured out step one."

Attending Del's Friday night Bible studies, Lonnie was from the neighborhood, living in the house behind his.

"Somebody just said, 'They're looking for a bass player, Christian or something,'" Lonnie remembered. "And I think that I talked to them and *we were all on the same page.*"

By "being on the same page," Lonnie meant that the vision of reaching lost souls would always be the priority. This project wasn't about fame or record deals, this was about pooling their resources and gifts to provide a greater impact in what they saw as a "Harvest" of souls.

"Yes, that's exactly right," Lonnie agreed. "And to me, that's how it would have to be. I just cared about having the Lord use me in any way He could so that people would come to know Him."

And that was their Covenant, Mike, Fred and Lonnie: they would play as long as they could preach and share Christ. If they couldn't do the latter, the former would have neither value nor purpose.

Mike mentioned, "I never met anybody like her. She's hard as rocks on some things and then soft as a pillow on others. I mean, she's just serious. She's linear, but creative, if that makes any sense."

There was no "wiggle room" with Lonnie. On anything. She was a different kind of "cat" and would serve as the group's conscience on more than one occasion, "*the Boys*" needing all the help they could get.

"My story is a little different," she said. "My parents, married almost 60 years, were both believers and I came to know the Lord about age five. My dad was a musician, played with big bands. I grew up with it. So, I had a very stable growing up.

But the Church part, it was a phony Methodist Church where I never heard the Gospel once. And so that was enough for me. I dropped out of the Church part."

Bound together by the shared vision of a music ministry and a general distrust of organized religion, the foundation for the new band was now set for Version 1.0, whatever they ended up calling themselves.

But what about Jeff?

"There was no sense that there wasn't room for Jeff to play," Mike suggested. "My sense was that Jeff didn't want to. He was already being recruited by guys at Azusa Pacific. The honest truth is, he was a better musician than any of us and had other opportunities."

Jeff was an excellent, highly sought-after musician and the "guys," to which Mike referred were *Thurlow Spurr and the Spurrlows*, a nationally established Gospel group. He would later hook up with Mr. Larnelle Harris. This change would be more than a consolation prize for Jeff, this was going to be a promotion.

And so, they began. Initially practicing in Fred's garage, it quickly became apparent that they were going to need several things: a bigger location, a repertoire and a whole lot of work, at the very top of the list.

"Sometimes we sounded better than others," Lonnie remembered, "but we always got to it. Sometimes we're playing and I'm thinking, 'We sound so bad,' but the Lord covered it all up. Sometimes things weren't quite in tune or it's not together or maybe it's time to stop for a quick prayer."

For the uninitiated, putting an original-music band together, of any kind, is a big deal. It's a grace-growing exercise not intended for the faint-hearted, especially when you're attempting something that's never been done before.

Under ordinary circumstances it takes a while to gel, to come together, to figure out who you are. Doing it for Jesus can add a whole new dimension of interest and complexity.

"Lord, how do we do this right?" Mike wondered. "How do we not kill each other? How do we present who you are and not what we are?"

Just as the nucleus for the band was forming, Del was coming to a decision about his Bible study. With crowds grown so large they spilled across East Dalton Avenue into Finkbiner Park, it was becoming too much.

But it wasn't just the crowds. Mary was hurting. "She had horrific headaches," Lonnie explained, "a result of being kicked in the head by a horse or mule as a child. She never complained but I knew she was suffering."

Ultimately, Del wasn't a Pastor; he was a Missionary. His home wasn't a Church; it was an outpost on the edge of the frontie˞ where he and Mary ministered to the wild-tribes gathering along the border.

More down to earth, and important to our story, is the fact that he had no intention of morphing a wildly-successful, Friday night Bible Study into a congregation, something that seemed all too common in those days.

After ministering to the burgeoning group of new disciples for only a few months, two things became clear to Del. The first was the depth of spiritual need in those who came to him and the second had to do with the limitations of his own calling.

Many good, even great people – people with greater gifts than Del Wilhite – have crashed and burned because they didn't possess the same kind of wisdom, born of humility and years. He'd done all he could.

"What I learned from Del was Biblical truth. He made it all so simple," Major reflected.

"His teaching was overwhelming. So far above our heads, yet somehow, we understood what he was teaching. He made the Bible come alive and helped me comprehend that God really loved me."

The best teachers do more than parrot well-rehearsed facts. The best teachers awaken the joy of learning within us. They excite our minds to dig, to connect the dots and dig deeper still. That was Del's role in their lives. It was that part of himself he left behind in each of them.

Mary passed away in 1983 and Del followed two years later. A reporter for the *Glendoran* wrote a final word for Del. "A warm, God-fearing man, with a positive belief in life and people, has left a legacy to mankind."

Del's legacy isn't trapped in the stone he fashioned or in anything he ever built. His legacy is discovered as we examine the fingerprints he left on the souls of the unwanted, those with whom organized religion would have nothing to do.

As a final act of love, Del recommended the Bethany Baptist Church where he and their evangelism buddies, Russ Chambers and Charley Eisenberg, were members. But it didn't work out; the other Church members were generally "aghast" at their appearance, as Mike remembered.

"They really didn't like us," Fred added, "because we were very different and had long hair. We wore Levi's, the girls wore Levi's, and we walked around barefooted."

Lacking the appropriate "outfits" and couture, the polite and ordinary conventions of Christendom seemed denied to them, excluding them from fellowship.

The truth of the matter was that America's churches would need some time to warm up to the idea of embracing the counter-culture. They'd been defending their hallowed grounds against such riffraff since the first brick was laid.

Events of the next 50 days would help provide clarity for all of our, now 18-year-old, contrarians. More Paul than Peter, they were in the process of learning that they weren't called to minister to the already Churched. It was becoming a hurtful education with the worst yet to come.

They were Evangelists, not *Revivalists* scheduling an annual Tour of Churches to remind Christians of their "first love." Their effective outreach would be to those who were most like themselves, those who Christians euphemistically refer to as, "the lost."

It was now early 1969. Drifting between Bible Studies and disastrous Church experiences, our newly-formed, Evangelical "posse," now 3 dozen zealots strong, was in need of a place to land.

The first Easter Sunday of their new lives was but a few months away; the first in which thoughts of "resurrection" assumed personal relevance; the first in which they viewed themselves as living parts of the ageless drama.

Between now and then, however, they'd have to survive a sneak attack from the Baptist Occupational Forces at the legendary, *Battle of Bellflower.*

Our fellowship of partially-civilized hooligans was about to be formally introduced to institutional Christianity, face down on a sidewalk.

"There are none so happy as new converts before they meet a theologian." [2]

---

[2] Anonymous

Del Wilhite

Del and "Mother Mary" Wilhite

Victims of Tradition

ob Harrington, dubbed "the Chaplain of Bourbon Street," was a well-known Evangelist during the 1960's and 70's. Spending most of his time working in the streets of New Orleans' French Quarter, "the nearest pocket of sin," he earned a reputation for shutting down bars and strip clubs by leading the owners to Christ.

Learning that Chaplain Bob was scheduled to speak at a prominent Baptist Church in Bellflower, about 25 miles south of Azusa, Charlie Eisenburg and Russ Chambers encouraged the group to attend. Sounding like something that was "right up their alley," everyone was onboard.

Mike picked up the story.

"And so, we all throw ourselves in some VW van and go down there, maybe 15 of us girls and guys and, you know how we looked. And I was in the back of the

Church with some of the girls who needed to use the bathroom back there.

And a guy walks by in a three-piece suit and says, 'Can I help you?'

And all lit up for God, we said, 'Oh, man, we came to hear the guy speak.' And he looks at us, no shoes, big hair, whatever. He says, 'Well, you're not dressed properly for the Sanctuary of the Lord.'

I had read the Book of Acts for the first time about a week before and, in all my wisdom, I said, 'Well, God doesn't dwell in temples made with hands.'

And I said, 'Who's this guy? Who cares?'

Well, he happens to be the Pastor of the Church. So, as we come from the back of the building to enter the sanctuary, there are five or six guys in powder-blue, leisure suits waiting for us; they looked like linebackers.

As we went *up* the stairs, they grabbed us and threw us *down* the stairs while the Pastor called the police. So, cop cars show up, helicopter shows up."

Listening to Mike tell the story I couldn't help but wonder how much the passing years may have embellished the tale. It didn't make sense that a church who sponsored an Evangelist specializing in work with street people would throw those very people back into the street.

But they all shared similar details.

Offering his insights, Jeff Newman remembered. "And we were going up the steps to go in and Debbie, which is my girlfriend at the time, was wearing culottes, which look like a skirt. But they're pants, right?

And the Deacon standing at the Sanctuary door says, 'You can't come in here.'"

Believing in the teens and their experience in Christ, Russ and Charlie were appalled that they weren't received into fellowship. New to religion, the group had never before seen Deacons argue; didn't know it was possible.

Jeff continued. "So. I'm standing there, just trying to figure out what's going on, and I look in and see the Chaplain getting ready to go on the platform. I'm looking at him, and he's got his hands up in the air because he can't do anything about it.

And so, what happens is that the Deacons kick into gear; they wouldn't let us in. Mike takes off his shoe, sits there and starts scraping the bottom of his shoe. And I thought, 'What's he doing?' You know what he's doing, right?

By the time we get to the parking lot, there are police everywhere, including helicopters with huge search lights. We're trapped in the parking lot and they're trying to figure out what happened. They thought there must be a panic. Anyway, they were just doing what cops do and then they found out that it was just a Church thing; *it's Christians.*"

Really?!

"There was no part of the local Church that wanted anything to do with us," Mike said. "And we weren't angry about it. We had zero hunger to be a part of the local Church." Go figure.

Placing ourselves in the moment, evangelical Christianity was at war with anything that resembled the counter-culture; anything resembling their interpretation of "the world, the flesh and the devil."

The Vietnam War was raging and our nation was being fractured along political and religious lines. Images of riots at the 1968 Democratic National Convention in Chicago, where you could tell the Patriots from the trouble-makers by the length of their hair, resonated with all "good" Americans.

Mingling their politics with their Faith, many Christians weren't prepared to accept hippie Believers without a change in their appearance. Reasoning that any "true" conversion would result in a spontaneous desire to comply, they saw themselves as Defenders of the Faith: *Bellflower Chapter.*

But, our pilgrims reasoned, there's a difference between unity and conformity. The former they supported but didn't feel the latter incumbent upon them. Jesus accepted them as they were; *"who are these people to deny us?"*

Re-enacting the New Testament rift over the place of Gentile savages in the newly-forming *ecclesia*, America's evangelical churches leaned toward risk aversion, erring on the side of caution.

What else could they do? *Victims of Tradition*, they shouldn't be faulted for being faithful to the light they had. Ritual creates its own, measured rhythm; a thousand generations finding comfort in its steady, predictable flow.

In hindsight, our teen-age believers all realized it was as much about attitude as it was sandals, culottes or jeans. They can laugh about it now.

But the Battle of Bellflower provides an accurate picture of the ecclesiastical opposition faced by all the counter-culture Christians. The resistance wasn't hope-inducing. It seemed a dead-end street.

Meanwhile, "the Band" was having some trouble finding a consistent place to rehearse. Russ Chambers found them an abandoned building in Glendora after they'd practiced at his home. Once. They also managed to rehearse at Bethany Baptist. Once.

But the idea was coming together: structure, sound, song-writing, all the ordinary things upon which collaborative musicians are focused. Perhaps more importantly, *the three of them* were coming together, figuring how they each fit as pieces of the puzzle.

One thing was clear from the beginning. Fred was going to lead, as Vocalist, Guitarist and song writer of whatever this musical experiment ended up being. For better or worse, as he went, so the band would go.

Having something to do with "the shoulders of giants," every musician who has ever lived built their sound borrowing from those they admire. Fred Caban was no exception.

When he first heard *Purple Haze*, Fred stuck his head inside his father's old, stereo console so he could pick up every nuance. "I was absolutely flabbergasted at what I heard. What an epiphany. It opened up a whole new world of music for me."

While he greatly admired Mr. Hendrix, and the revelation of sound he introduced, Fred's style was actually somewhere between Jimi and Mike Bloomfield. His first exposure to 1968's *Super Session* album, with Mike Bloomfield, Al Kooper and Steven Stills, influenced his solos as much as Mr. Hendrix influenced his style.

Throw in a smattering of the "San Francisco Sound," occasional influences reminiscent of the Doors and

Jefferson Airplane, add the power of Clapton's *Cream* and Hendrix' *Experience,* and you'll find the musical furrow that Fred, Mike and Lonnie were inclined to plow.

With Del out of the picture, and no desire to keep getting thrown out of the area Churches, the group continued to meet with Ray Salmon in a dorm room at Azusa College. That's where they met fellow APC student, Ron Turner.

Described by band members as "relentless; a bull in a China shop; a force of nature," Ron Turner was one of those people who had a knack for making things happen. Quoting *ZZ Top,* "takin' care of business was his name." [1]

A fierce proponent of the old adage, "It's easier to ask forgiveness than to get permission," there was an insistence about Ron. Some folks interpreted that energy as pushiness but it wasn't that. The passion with which he embraced faith and ministry was intense, spilling out onto everyone he met. For some people, the characteristic was laudable. For others, it was a problem.

Walking into the Hollywood First Presbyterian Church at age 13, with his 9-year-old sister clinging to his hand, Ron grew up under the tutelage of Pastor Don Williams. Eventually serving there as a youth minister

---

[1] "Jesus Just Left Chicago." ZZ Top, *Tres Hombres*, 1973

between 1960 and 1965, Ron Turner's trajectory was fixed early.

Eight years older than Mike and Fred, he was converted in 1960 toward the end of his Senior Year at Hollywood High School. Preaching, passing out Gospel tracts he'd created and writing the words, "God is love" in felt pen on his white T-shirts, Ron Turner was a living Billboard for Jesus.

About to graduate from Azusa Pacific College with a B.A., he would later earn his first Master's Degree from the Haggard School of Theology and a Master's of Divinity from Fuller Theological Seminary. Easily provoked to laughter, his effervescent and pervasive sense of humor was sometimes misinterpreted. Sarcasm wasn't his "long suit."

Asking Ron about his first impression of the musicians he joked, "It looked like their barber died."

Jeff Newman was clear on their first meeting. "I remember Ron pulling us together. He saw our instruments and asked, 'Hey, do you guys play music?' And I said, yeah."

"Well, I want you to come to Huntington Beach, man."

Now serving as the youth minister at the Arcadia Community Church, Ron took his Youth Group to Huntington Beach every Sunday for Communion. In a church of 60 elderly people, his group consisted of "about five Grammar School kids, three Junior High kids, and about two or three High School kids."

Ron had nowhere to go but up.

After jumping at the opportunity to play, Jeff and the others tried to figure out what they were going to do. "We're wondering, 'How does this go? We don't have any songs.'"

So, they decided to make it up as they went along.

Listening to their obviously extemporaneous effort, further aggravated by the intensity of their preferred volume levels, it didn't take long for Ron to respond.

"He unplugs the music and yells, '*Stop playing!* Just *say* something,'" Jeff remembered.

Ron didn't know what to make of it.

Commenting on that moment, he reflected, "They shared with me that they wanted to take their music as a rock group and share their kind of music for Jesus.

I did not understand it the first time. It took me a little bit of time to grasp the rock part of it. I came to know and understand rock music through Agape."

Whatever he was expecting, it wasn't this. If there was any hope of a long-term connection, all of them would be forced to stretch themselves. He didn't understand them; they didn't understand him. They would figure it out.

Picking up his narrative about the beach, Jeff added, "So we just started talking to the kids, just like we did when we got baptized. 'All you kids, you need to get right with God.' We start preaching, right?

So, we're learning as we go along: 'This is how you do it.' That's how we learned to share our faith. You do it a couple of times and pretty soon, man, wow, *'We can do this!'*"

Observing the overall positive results with his youth group, Ron invited the band members to attend a Sunday service at his Church.

"So, we went to the Arcadia Community Church," Jeff noted, "and met these people who seemed very nice and sweet. But, bro, they were looking at us with funny eyeballs.

In the youth group, it's like you have these kids who loved us, and their parents thinking, 'Oh, my God, it's the Antichrist or something.' They're freaking out."

Though it took Jesus three years to wear out his welcome with religious leaders, our over-achievers managed it in less than four weeks. Receiving an ultimatum from the Church, Ron informed the group: "Well, guys, we didn't clean up fast enough for them."

"And that's when we decided." Jeff said. "We decided, as a group, that we were going to become a Church."

It was easy for them to make that decision. None of them had serious responsibilities. But it was different for Ron. He wouldn't leave his position of ministry to gamble his future on a group of 18-year-olds he'd known less than six weeks. At least, not voluntarily.

Evidence of tradition gone wrong, Ron was told to leave; "and take your long-haired friends with you," Ron's wife, Eila, remembered.

An article in *The Agape Banquet*, a publication later produced by the Church in the Park, attempted to explain the issue and the beginnings of Agape. The wording inspired both admiration and skepticism.

"These young people, looking for God, so offended the church that they fired Ron without warning. Fifty churches refused Ron as a youth minister because of a fear and distaste for children with long hair."

While being turned down by a handful of Churches may say something about the will of God, being turned down by "50 churches" likely says something about the candidate. Ron seemed the proverbial "square peg," never quite the right fit for his beloved Presbyterian Church. Perhaps the "accept us as we are" hippies might extend him the same grace.

Ron had also been conducting a Wednesday night Bible Study on the open lawn behind the Library at Azusa Pacific for about 10 months. The decision to start an independent Church was announced at the next meeting. Ron told the group, now approaching 50 - 60 people, that he would be willing to help start a church by preaching and serving Communion.

Citing the Battle of Bellflower as an example, he told the gathered group of disenfranchised youth, "If you can't find a church that will accept you, we will."

But what were they going to call this thing, this indie caravan of dust-shaking, attitude-challenged, self-exiles?

Intent on building a "Book of Acts Church," they chose the Greek word, ἀγάπη (agápē) Agape, speaking of God's non-discriminating, unconditional love for all mankind. Beyond emotion, it embraces a deep and profound, sacrificial love that transcends circumstance.

"You cannot be bad enough to make God love you less," they believed, "and you cannot be good enough to make Him love you more." That was their message. That was their product. That was their identity.

Lacking any sense of "branding," Mike mentioned, "The original suggestion for the name was *Eros to Agape*, which is, from romantic, human love to God's love."

"I don't know that it matters," Mike stated, "but I'll take credit for that." Becoming sarcastic, he joked, "It was my idea, based out of my deep knowledge of the Greek language."

Like any self-respecting Bible student, Mike was enamored with his own, Greek studies and had the Concordances to prove it.

Whoever forwarded the ideas, they all embraced them body and soul. With one mind, vision and purpose, the musicians would be known as Agape and the fellowship would be known as *the Church in the Park*.

Ron would be the Pastor and Chief Architect of the Church, responsible for preaching, teaching and over-seeing an already growing body of believers. Agape, the band, would be the strong, evangelistic arm, drawing crowds to be reached and taught for Christ.

"None of us were public speakers," Fred reflected. "We were young kids. We thought it was kind of cool that Ron would come on stage and speak when we were done."

Neither Lonnie, Fred nor Mike saw the band as obsequious to Ron s ministry but as equal partners and necessary to the success of the entire enterprise. Though time would reveal that Ron may have had a different sense of things, another great synergy was now brought to life.

Whatever was good for the Fellowship was good for Agape and vice-versa. Whatever hurt one, hurt the other. They would come to need each other. Ron would help them book gigs and, as "fishers of men," Agape would show up to provide the nets.

Like all the disconnected groups and cells of the nascent Jesus Movement, they believed that "the best way to predict the future is to create it." Church Planting became the universal vison, the "new wine" finally grown weary of the old bottles, not by choice but by natural chemistry.

But there was one thing the newly energized group hadn't factored into their equations. While Ron Turner was a great many, wonderful things – father, teacher, evangelist, organizer and "killer" promoter among them – by his own admission, he wasn't a Pastor.

Describing the moment of his "calling" at age 19, Ron stated, "I'm praying, 'What do you want me to do with my life, Jesus?' And I take the Bible and throw it over a few pages, like a big, thick amount. BOOM! And it lands in Second Timothy, chapter four. I glance down at it and turn the pages back the other way."

In an effort to double-check with Heaven, Ron again employed a random-flip of the pages. What do you think? There it was again. Bordering on superstition, Christians would likely abandon the technique if it did not, so often, provide comfort.

"It just said, clearly, '*Do the work of an evangelist* and fulfill thy ministry.' [2] I wrote in my Bible, '2/19/ 61, calling to go into the ministry,' and I believe that was what God wanted me to do."

Pastor, Teacher, Evangelist, Apostle or Prophet, a person's calling can matter greatly in such moments, especially when it comes to things like expectations, communication styles and inter-personal skills.

Calling and vision are closely related. Both may be described as a benevolent impulse, gently gnawing at the root of our imagination and thought processes. It's "deep calling unto deep," the connection being made in a human mind. It's an aligning of Kingdom needs and human gifts.

Those sustained impulses are often interpreted by Christians as any variation of the will, voice or Spirit of God. For mission-minded people, they are to be followed, like connecting invisible dots.

Evangelists and Apostles follow one set of impulses; Pastors and Teachers follow their own. Prophets, whoever they may be, operate on a unique set of rhythms. The impulses that each follow are consistent with the needs of their vision. Apostles build. Prophets know. Evangelists recruit. Teachers elevate. Pastors nurture.

---

[2] 2nd Timothy 4:5

Ron knew all of that. He wasn't trying to blur lines, and starting a church certainly wasn't on his radar. "I was just trying to meet a need for people," he said.

"The Holy Spirit really touched me deep and the power of their music was like, unbelievable. I mean, it sounds crazy, but it was that powerful for me. It was that radical.

And I felt goosebumps all over my body and felt like I wanted to be involved with them. But I was going to leave very shortly, in September, to become a Presbyterian Minister."

Following in the footsteps of many of his spiritual heroes, those who'd gone into ministry from Hollywood Presbyterian Church, Ron had just received a letter of acceptance, with a full scholarship, from Princeton Theological Seminary.

Praying mightily about the possible change to his long-cherished plans, Ron's mind visualized a "picture of Jesus walking into a park, a public park, talking with people and, as they gathered around him, he began to share.

So, I called the guys up the next day and shared the vision of the public park and they said, 'Covina Park would be good' and we could meet at the band shell that already had benches for about 500."

It was all too natural. Working with street people in 1966, on the streets of Helsinki, Finland, with his new wife, Eila, Ron was already in touch with a counter-culture expression rivaling that of Haight-Ashbury.

While none of them would have identified themselves as part of a "Movement" or even a revival, they felt themselves being moved forward by God's spirit. Their first, real effort at seeking the specific will of God, they simply moved in the rhythm of the moment. They were kids. What did they know?

Unconcerned about the theological ramblings of writers or critics, religious classifications or nomenclature, the rejected hippies and their rejected cleric just wanted to be like Jesus, doing what He did, spreading the love of Heaven.

Innocence is such a lovely place to begin.

"Behold, a Sower went forth to sow....."

Fred Caban

Mike Jungman

Lanore "Lonnie" Campbell

Ron Turner

In the Beginning

When was the last time you did something for the first time? The last time you risked everything for something invisible? The last time you stood, "on the edge of a feather," and actually expected to fly? [1]

For our burgeoning troop of believers, *this* was one of those extraordinary kinds of days.

Without bulletins, song books, bands or worship teams, they placed a mic in front of Fred and his acoustic guitar. Singing praise songs for about 15-20 minutes, Ron introduced the first Communion of their new adventure.

Preaching a Communion "message" for about 30 minutes, he pronounced a loving warning to those about to participate.

---

[1] Neil Young, "Expecting to Fly." 1967

Emphasizing that you shouldn't take the bread or the cup if you weren't a disciple, it left the impression that bad things could happen if you transgress the order of things. Such pronouncements weren't unusual in Evangelical churches but *they'd* never heard it like that.

It was suddenly, serious business.

Following the same Liturgical presentation used on the Beach with the Arcadia Youth Group, it was all part of who Ron Turner was: a theologically trained Presbyterian. The fact that he hooked up with such rebels and non-conformists in the first place seems a small wonder in itself.

Walking into the crowd, Ron handed a large, glass goblet to the first person in each row. He and Eila had been collecting them for a while.

"We used to get gasoline, like for twenty-one cents a gallon," Ron laughed. "And I would pull into these gas stations out in Burbank that, when you bought so many gallons, you got a goblet. And we kept collecting them, put them in a box every time we got gas."

Drinking from those large, customer-loyalty collectables, each passed it down the row until all were served. Sitting in silence, each person broke a piece of bread from a common loaf, and passed it to the next person, waiting until all were served.

"And then I preached the Word for about one hour," he remarked.

For several hours, the celebration of joy in Covina Park firmly convinced all of them that they were heading in the right direction. This could work!

As the Fellowship continued its pace of rapid growth, Ron developed the structure using what he'd learned at the First Presbyterian Church in Hollywood from his close friend, Dr. Henrietta Mears.

One of the founders of the *National Sunday School Association*, she grew the church's Sunday School program from 400 to 6,500 in two years. Later founding her own publishing company, "Gospel Light," she also founded *Forest Home*, a Christian conference center outside Big Bear, California.

Profoundly impacting the ministries of people like Bill Bright, Billy Graham and Louis Evans Jr., Dr. Mears is believed by many theologians to have shaped Bill Bright's Four Spiritual Laws that eventually defined modern evangelism in the 20th century.

The group was building on good, solid ground.

To his credit, Ron was attempting to "harmonize the variety," to blend those who followed from his study group, Arcadia Community and Bethany Baptist with the irreverent and magnetic Azusa outlaws.

Borrowing from Doctor Mears' proven methods and printed materials, he developed a system designed to promote steady growth and chain-of-command.

Identifying, and then selecting from the congregation, those who appeared to be the existing, natural leaders, Ron formed the FMs, the Future Ministers.

Personally tutored by Ron, they helped with many of the community's needs including the serving of Communion to a perpetually growing, outdoor crowd of many hundreds.

As genuine as they were zealous, and as eager to learn as they were to tell somebody about it, the FMs joyfully picked up every wonderful detail Ron was laying down. Pouring himself into them, the young ministers-in-training became the biggest supporters of his straight-forward, non-sugar-coated approach to ministry and life. Going forward, the FMs were generally viewed as the "Inner Circle."

Expanding the mid-week Bible studies, Ron selected leaders and co-leaders, and assigned them to groups of less than 12 people. Each of them was to meet with every member of their group for one hour per week. "For fellowship, to see how they were doing in their life and to pray with them," Ron wrote.

Every few weeks, Leaders and Co Leaders met with Ron where they could "share with me any confidential issues in the life of their group if they felt it necessary." Lest the cynic wonder, Ron wasn't looking for dirt. He was attempting to model, and build, a caring community of Christian thinkers and artists.

Embracing the same Book by Book, verse-by-verse regimen observed by many churches with a large influx of new converts, Bible studies tended to be an all-night affair.

The leaders met with their groups for the first hour going over the material from the previous week to get everyone up to speed on what Ron was teaching next. The second hour, the groups gathered, sang a few songs and Ron taught until he was done. Fellowship generally followed.

With a congregation populated with 100 part-time evangelists and a dynamic music ministry, they now had a sustainable, organized plan for reaching and teaching their Community for Christ.

Within eight months, their combined efforts grew the church to more than 300 regular attendees in Covina Park. With what seemed like spectacular, daily growth, the Agape Fellowship was but another reflection of what God was doing across Southern California.

Likely disappointing to the preachers, most of those attending at Covina Park weren't there for the weekly Communion service or the in-depth, mid-week Bible studies. Most were there for the electric congregation, for the energetic *Fellowship of Discovery* in like minds.

Highly infectious, that common dynamic brought identifiable vitality to the entire Jesus Movement.

Completely apart from their connection to Christ, people were falling in love with something they'd never had before – a purpose and a cause larger than themselves.

One year out of High School, looking for work and "needing something to hang on to," Ed Shorer followed an attractive face he met at the Employment Agency to Sunday morning in Covina Park. He was a bit apprehensive, "because I'm Jewish." Christianity wasn't something that would make his family happy.

When asked what he thought about the music of Agape and Ron's teaching, Ed laughed and said, "Well, I'm going to use my current family motto: it was 'Good Enough.'"

Like hundreds of others, Ed wasn't there for the music, the teaching or a pretty face. Well, maybe for the pretty face. Ed's primary reason for attending services in Covina Park was shared by the majority of disenfranchised youth who found their way to the group. They embraced the Agape Fellowship because of the energy, creativity and overflow of joy that made them feel welcome.

With flowers in their hair and incense in the air, their "Scarborough Fair" notion of family and community was like nectar to blind bees. It bound them together.

As if he didn't have enough to do with the church as a whole, Ron was true to his commitment to schedule gigs for the band, keeping them busy.

Playing at every Public Park in a 30-mile radius, as well as High School auditoriums and public concourses at several of the area colleges, it seemed amazing to Fred, Mike and Lonnie. Almost too good to be true.

They had no idea that Ron was setting up "rogue" performances, and that the good fortune was actually, "guerilla warfare." They weren't actually invited to play in many of these places but, apparently, that didn't matter.

It turns out, Ron's enthusiasm wasn't obstructed by formalities. Things like getting permits, permission or approval for the band to play never held him back. While he would later connect with friends in colleges, high schools and universities to schedule some great events, his early efforts were deemed sketchy.

Mike, Lonnie and street-evangelism friend, Sharron Bassett, offered insights.

"We'd show up at local state colleges and he literally says, 'Where's the band plug in?' and people look at each other and say, 'Over there.' So, we go and play."

Mike continued, "He would pretty much run over whoever was in the way. And his justification, of course, was that, 'We're here to preach the Gospel.' So, we all kind of went, 'Oh wow, really?"

Reminding them of the unannounced invasions they'd shared with David Berg's, *Teens for Christ*, they threw up their gear, fired up a generator and flexed their collective will. Without the need for permission or an electrical outlet, they were free to play anywhere "the Lord led."

"There was more than one gig that we didn't know about," Lonnie offered. As an example, she said, "We were in the middle of a Common area at UCLA, like right in the middle so that people would be walking through it during lunch. That's when I learned about it. And we did that several times."

Sharron Bassett added, "I remember sneaking underneath the driveway gates that lifted up to let you onto the campus. They just set up and played."

There were many who admired Ron's boldness. They liked the fact that nothing in this world, not propriety, convention, preference or Law deterred him from forwarding the Cause of Christ. "Ron was a risk taker for the Gospel," one of them wrote me. "Why would we let a little red tape stop us from saving lives?" [2]

To those good folks, Ron Turner was almost Apostolic.

---

[2] Richard Greenburg

Meanwhile, after working through some of Fred's first songs, Agape got the chance to play their first, "big-deal" gig.

"Ron had a connection at the Salt Company out in Hollywood. We didn't have a place to sleep, so we slept in my car," Mike remembered.

Playing until midnight on Halloween, 1969, they shared the stage with Larry Norman who had just released his first so o-album.

Listening to Agape play, Larry became animated and showed great interest in what they were doing.

"He came out of his chair because, 'Look at these wild kids. They're playing loud Hendrix type music and sharing Jesus.'" Mike remembered. "He seemed blown away that, *what we were doing* could be done."

Larry Norman was impressed enough to discuss getting Agape into a studio immediately, within the next few days. Already past midnight, Larry also invited Fred to spend the night at his apartment, within walking distance from the Salt Company.

An unusual and unheralded moment in the history of Christian Rock, the meeting between two of the earliest "Pioneers" of what was to come, Larry and Fred shared their visions and music through the night.

Imagine Kit Carson and Jim Bridger meeting at the annual *Mountain Man Rendezvous* in Wyoming, "swappin' yarns 'n tellin' lies." Two rough-cut individualists, working late into an October night, pushing back on musical frontiers while everyone else was still looking for the mountain.

Talking about it, Fred said, "I spent the night with him before we actually went into the studio. And he was looking at some of my lyrics, kind of working on stuff, and then he gave me suggestions that would make my songs better."

The power and liberty of Agape's music was indeed attractive to Larry because it was unique to his Christian, musical experience. Seeing them as a "diamond in the rough," Larry hoped he could help Fred modify his lyrics.

Setting up his recorder and microphone, Larry began to go over the songs Fred felt the band was ready to record.

"I would sing and then he'd sing and get ideas."

Going back and forth through the night, the four songs, "Happy," "Man," "Trust" and "Blood," found their way onto Larry Norman's recorder.

"We, kind of, stumbled on a couple of things," Fred mentioned. "Larry would say, 'Well, you know, this might be better if you did it this way, or if you did it that way.' He was focused on my lyrics."

Larry Norman was a poet who put his verse to song. Fred Caban was a Lead Guitarist for whom lyrics had always been a necessary evil. As a musical evangelist, however, the words were now the only thing that mattered. But he didn't have much experience at the task.

Viewing his music as an audio Gospel tract, Fred demonstrated no interest in a "Dylan-esque" lilt to his message. Simple, to the point and easy to back up with Scripture, the words had a Divine origin for Fred. To him, they were near sacred.

"And I said, 'Larry, God gave me these lyrics. I *can't* change them. Not even if you think, from a songwriting standpoint, they would be better. From a spiritual standpoint, they were given to me just the way I order them. And so, even though they might not sound good lyrically, spiritually, *I can't change them.'*

Some songwriters view collaboration as a boon, fully embracing the notion that the surrender of ego and exchange of skills can further develop their music. Curious about the possibility of making the final song "greater than the sum of its parts," musicians involved tend to stretch themselves during the process.

Others view their art as near sacred, the original inspiration being the only thing that matters. For such artists, things like collaboration, compromise and control all occupy the same space.

"Larry was kind of set back by that," Fred observed, "but I had to stand my ground. Then I asked everybody to come on down and told them that Larry was going to record us in the studio the next day."

Describing a dusty, run-down recording space somewhere in Hollywood, Fred, Mike and Lonnie jumped into the moment like 10-year-olds on a new trampoline. Taking the entire event as a "good sign," they didn't notice that they were now more excited than Larry Norman.

Fred remembered, "After he recorded us, I never heard from him after that. We didn't get tapes; we didn't get nothin'. I figured he was working on our album or something. Then, just all of a sudden, he wasn't there; he wasn't available. I never talked to him again.

We played with Larry at various concerts but, even there, we never really talked. He just disappeared."

Misunderstanding his intent, relative to his interest in their music, bandmembers were disappointed. But the fact is, Larry Norman was on a mission, interested in signing Christian Rock musicians to his newly emerging *One Way Records* label. Otherwise, his dance card seemed full.

Shortly after the recordings, on New Year's Eve, 1969, Agape again shared the stage with Larry Norman at the Pasadena Civic Auditorium. According to reports from bandmembers, he ignored them completely; he never spoke to them.

Backstage, however, something unexpected and far more significant than a social "slight" was being formulated. Lonnie came to a very difficult decision. Several years older than "the Boys," her first child had been born in September.

"We were playing and my daughter was in the baby buggy backstage. We were loud and I was thinking, 'This is so bad because it's almost midnight and this is bad.' They were starting to travel all over and it's not a good job traveling all over the place.

My dad played with big bands but I didn't realize it when I was young. That's because he stopped when we were born. And that's the reason it's not a family business. So, I just thought, 'This is bad.' So, I dropped out of Agape."

For herself, Lonnie wasn't happy about it. The first female bass player in the history of Christian Rock, she loved being an integral part of a music ministry that was seeing some amazing results. But, with crystal clarity, she knew where her first loyalties lay.

"I didn't bring a child into the world to turn her over to a baby sitter," she told me. Her conscience and strong sense of responsibility wouldn't allow Lonnie to leave her child with anyone but family or expose her to the rising decibels of Rock 'n Roll fury.

Though Lonnie stayed on through Spring Break concerts in Palm Springs, the path was clear. God was preparing better things for Lonnie Campbell Bissell and bigger things for Fred Caban and Mike Jungman.

It was now early 1970. Amy Grant was 9 years old. Matthew Ward, of *the 2nd Chapter of Acts,* was 11.

Mylon LeFevre signed with Columbia Records and formed the old-school, Southern Rock group, the "Holy Smoke Doo Dah Band."

Chuck Girard and Tommy Coomes ended their wanderings and launched *Love Song* at Calvary Chapel. Codifying the sound that would eventually become the pattern for Contemporary Christian Music, they would become the most enduring of all the early pioneers.

In Ohio, Grammy Award winning guitarist Phil Keaggy accepted Christ following the death of his mother. Within a few months, members of the All Saved Freak Band would conduct Bible studies in a house he shared with other musicians in Kent: "The house on Summit Street."

By now, the Jesus Movement was starting to find acceptance in the two, disparate camps of Evangelical Christianity and American culture. An article in *Time Magazine* titled, "the Jesus Revolution," featured a pop-art picture of Jesus on its front cover.

Not to be outdone, Life magazine ran an article in their May, 1971, issue, "The Groovy Christians." It was becoming "Hip" to talk about Jesus.

In a recorded interview, David Wilkerson estimated there were 300,000 people in the JPM by the early 1970s.[3] Though there is no way of confirming such numbers, it was becoming abundantly clear that God was stirring the entire nation and people were starting to notice.

Ed Stetzer, *Chair of Church, Mission and Evangelism* at Wheaton College declared that the Jesus Movement "represented the Fourth Great Awakening; the Fourth Wave of revival in American history."

Reinventing religious space, the "Movement" marched away from the Coast. Popping up in places like Boise, Idaho and Waterloo, Iowa, everyday America was now being exposed to the revival.

Meanwhile, back in Azusa, Fred and Mike were in need of another bass player. Since Jack Bruce already had a gig with Eric Clapton, he was going to be unavailable. But, if they could get somebody like that, someone with a fluid style and big sound, that would be just about right.

---

[3] "The Jesus People Movement: 50+ Years Later," Oscar Merlo, June 17, 2020, *Talbot Magazine*

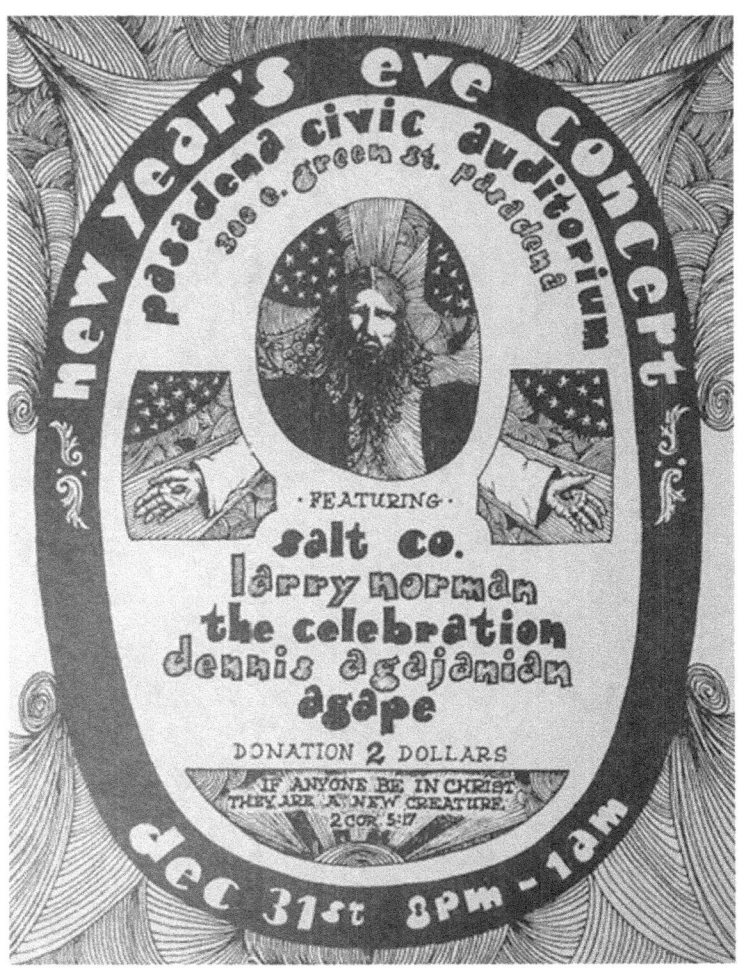

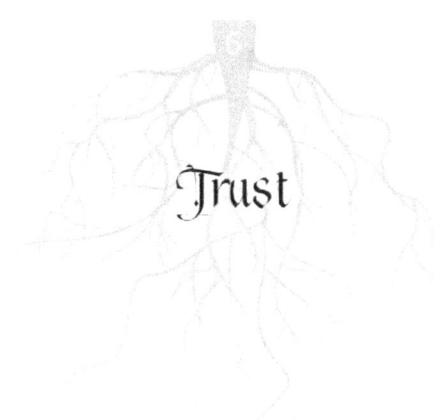

Trust

Known to Fred and Mike since he was the bassist for their High School rivals, "The Soundproof Cookie Jar," John Peckhart's musical hero was Jack Bruce. Nice coincidence! Fred, rather prejudicially, opined, "He was just as good and even used the same kind of bass, you know, the whole nine yards. He definitely improved the whole, rhythmic aspect of our band."

While Lonnie had been a rock solid, on-the-beat bassist, John's dalliance with Lead Guitar afforded him a much more fluid style. His fills between beats and measures opened up what some reviewers heard as a more, "Progressive" sound.

As important as his "chops," his musical instincts were more closely aligned with Mike and Fred than Lonnie. While she knew where they were, every beat and measure, John knew where they wanted to go.

As part of the Covina Park church, John had been to several Agape concerts and had a pretty good idea of what they were doing. The fact that the music was primarily Blues made it almost instinctual to seasoned Rock musicians.

Taking only a few weeks to get up to speed, his style of play provided the missing link, providing a deeper groove, taking Fred and Mike closer to the sound they envisioned. With more punch and authority, the music now had a flexible backbone.

Work began on the first album, almost immediately.

After being turned down by a few Christian producers who really didn't know what to make of their hard rock sound, Ron approached local studio producer and APC music professor, Marlin Jones.

Marlin contacted Wally Duguid, who also worked with Barry McGuire, 2nd Chapter of Acts and Keith Green to do the Engineering.

Offering free studio time between midnight and 6:00am at *Abbey Sound Studio* in Hollywood, Marlin helped Agape record their first album, *Gospel Hard Rock*. With roughly 20 hours of studio time, they churned out ten, roughly recorded songs.

Mike quipped, "The first album we did in the middle of the night, *sounds* like it was done in the middle of the night."

Fred's comments were similar. "Our first album was pretty tacky but we didn't know what we were doing and the engineer had never recorded a loud rock band before. He didn't know how to mic everything so that's how things came out."

When recording Rock music, the engineer always begins with things like microphone choice, for vocals and instruments, followed by the placement and angle of the mics. A fair amount of studio time is then required to establish the peak volume levels necessary for clean reproduction. They don't call them "Engineers" for nothing.

But the configurations and specs used for people like Pat Boone, Dale Evans, John Fischer or Barry McGuire weren't going to work for Agape or any power-trio, anywhere.

Distortion? On purpose? Really!?

Like Marlin and Wally, many of the faculty members at Azusa Pacific College were moved by the eruption of evangelism among their own students. And they were eager to support it.

Dr. Cornelius Haggard, President of Azusa Pacific College wrote for *The Agape Banquet*,

"I feel that the Agape Ministry is the most exciting missionary ministry to young people in America today. In a period when young people were turning from materialism and secularism, and seeking for a spiritual experience, Agape came into being to challenge them from drugs, sex and drink to a spiritual experience in Christ."

The growing recognition, from people who mattered, caused everyone to feel like Steve Martin's character of Navin R. Johnson in the movie, *The Jerk*. Seeing his name in a phone book for the very first time, Navin danced through the parking lot yelling deliriously,

"I'm *somebody* now!"

Two years from stumbling into Jesus, our bohemian believers were now considered legit. Important people said so. Incorporating the fledgling work under the name, *International Agape Ministries*, IAM, they were poised for good things.

But frictions between band members and Ron started to grow as they felt he was assuming too much, taking too much control. Professional musicians, they'd bargained for a promoter and booking agent, believing they could manage their own affairs.

But Ron was the designated grown-up, convinced he needed to take a personal hand in their growth.

"I was driving my car with the guys, Fred, Mike and maybe Jeff. We were going down the street and there were some kids on the sidewalk and they yelled out the window, 'God loves you!'

I drove about 100 more feet, pulled over and said, 'Wait a minute, you don't yell out the window! Do you want to go back and share Christ?

Don't shout out the window! It's insulting! I don't want to turn people off to God because of our immaturity.'"

Talking to me about it, Ron added, "There was this morality in me and God was always working. I was always correcting. I hate to say that."

It was that, "always correcting" part that started to wear thin with the teen-agers. Immature and childlike in the faith, they had no idea that Jesus would be upset about their unbridled enthusiasm. Though they pardoned Ron's rough edges by owning, "His heart was in the right place," the continual corrections began to create distance between them.

Fred offered, "He started pushing his way to being the manager and stuff. And I think at that point, we began to have issues with him and with us playing where we were playing."

It was one thing to play for free. They never thought twice about that, seeing it as an opportunity to win souls. But it was another thing altogether to feel awkward about it, wondering if the authorities would show up and pull the plug.

Is that what Jesus required?

"When Ron started to take over, it was hard for me to roll with it but he was also the promoter. He set up all the gigs and managed the money," Mike added.

Ron's methodologies, as a Booking Agent and a leader, were starting to trouble them. But band members felt stuck. He was also their Pastor and this was *their* ministry, as well. At least they felt that way. They had the bear by the tail and the only option was to hold on.

Jeff Newman and several others continued to work in the streets with Russ Chambers and Charlie Eisenberg, the Baptist Deacons who befriended them early in their experience. Handing him a tract, "How to be filled with the Holy Spirit," Jeff took it seriously. These men had never misled him before.

"I don't think they knew what was in it," Jeff said, "because I took it home and read it. And in my bedroom, after reading it, I invited the Holy Spirit to come into me. And I mean, it was explosive. My gosh, man, this is real!

It was just like getting saved bro. I say better. I don't know what you call it.

After that event, I went to the Bible study with Ron, and I'm bustin', I'm blowin' up. I said, 'What we all need here is the Baptism of the Holy Spirit.'

Oh, man, he just sat there and rebuked me: 'You're out of order and in confusion.'"

"We're not charismatic," Ron told them. "I didn't hold back on being critical of the things I thought were fake."

Jeff continued, "I gave him all five accounts of the Holy Spirit coming in Acts. He couldn't answer it. All he could say is, 'The Church Fathers don't believe in that.'

Sounding like echoes of Mike Jungman at *the Battle of Bellflower,* Jeff responded, "The Church Fathers? Who are those guys? Maybe they know more about this than the Apostles. I just know the Book of Acts."

Following the public rebuke and "dressing-down," Jeff wrestled with his own, profound experience. After pondering long over the issue, he finally concluded, "I guess I was wrong. But how can you deny the experience I had?"

Richard Lopez shed additional light on the subject.

Nine-years-old when his older brother, Philip, jammed in their family garage with Agape members, Richard was the person who coined the phrase, "the San Gabriel Boys."

"The Holy Spirit Movement isn't what Ron was teaching," Richard offered. "He warned everyone to avoid going to places that practiced it. Ron called out people in the crowd that starting believing in the Baptism, telling them to leave and not return. I was escorted to my car and told to not come back."

There is no doubt that the *Seven Gifts of the Spirit*[1] were in operation in Agape and Ron Turner. But the Baptism in the Holy Spirit, and the gift of tongues, is a completely different subject. Dividing faithful believers since the first day of Pentecost, there was no place for it at the Church in the Park.

To many, Ron seemed to be turning an authoritarian corner. To many others, he was "the most genuine man I've ever met." Compensating for the tension that can arise from such polar opposites of opinion, we're yet left to conclude that Ron's impulses didn't always display his best.

Neither do mine.

Since Ron's training, experience and natural impulses identified such "outbursts" as excess and error, his instinct was to protect these young believers from heresy. As much a lapse of wisdom as a flash of malice, the manner in which the correction was carried out remains the lasting memory for all. Ron felt that he was just doing his ecclesiastical job.

But the interaction with Ron caused Jeff to stumble. If he'd been so wrong about this, what else had he been

---

[1] 1 Corinthians 12:1-11

wrong about? Doubting himself and all of his experiences for the first time, Jeff began to wonder.

Trust had been shaken. Who could he believe?

"When he talked me out of it, man, that was a bummer anyway. Denying the experience began to cause all different kinds of doubt to come into my head."

Jeff Newman, Richard Lopez and several others left over the issue.

Among those who'd been with Ron the longest, those who knew him as someone other than, "the guy who breaks bread on Sunday morning," relationships were being tested.

Lonnie and Bob also decided it was time for them to move on. Much more conservative than their hippie brethren, there were also "some theological differences between Bob and Ron," she offered.

By then, Lonnie had become a "Pillar" for many of the younger women of the Covina Park Fellowship. Jeff Newman's sister, Sharon, made mention of the role Lonnie filled in their community.

"We grew up in turbulent times back then, potential prey to multiple social predators. Lonnie Campbell watched over the young women in our fellowship like a mother hen. She remains a strong, intelligent, honorable and courageous role model in my heart."

With the congregation coalescing around the wound, and their first album to promote, Ron and the band adjusted their trajectories to maintain their common focus on evangelism.

"We were playing all the time," Mike told me. "From here to Colorado, to Oregon, to everywhere in western Arizona; all over. There were as many as five nights a week. We played at High Schools during the week, maybe two or three, and then had concerts on the weekend where everybody from those schools were invited."

Ministering through the Summer and Fall of 1970, Agape scheduled a special New Year's Eve concert in Pasadena, the night before *the Tournament of Roses Parade.*

Ron contacted the administration of Fuller Theological Seminary about using one of the properties they owned in Pasadena, a parking lot about a half-block from the parade route on Orange Grove Boulevard.

Mike commented, "Everybody in southern California knows where the party is on New Year's. Hot-rodders, cruising down the street, people sleeping all over the sidewalks. It was a big, all-night party."

Playing there made perfect sense. That's where the people were, that's where they needed to be. Bob Harrington's model declared that the nearest Christian to a "pocket of sin," automatically becomes its missionary.

Street closures along the Parade route went into effect at 10:00 pm on New Year's Eve. Along Colorado Blvd., from Orange Grove Blvd. to Sierra Madre Blvd., and northbound on Sierra Madre to Paloma, everything shuts down.

Overnight camping is permitted on the sidewalks for New Year's Eve but, if you wanted a good position, you had to stake your claim by Noon of the 31st. By shut down time, the streets are rockin' beyond repair.

Arriving to set up their gear just before the 10:00pm street closures, Fred, Mike and John were greeted with occasional rain drops and gusting winds that proved mildly problematic

"I thought how cool it looked in the lights when you hit cymbals with rain on them; kind of psychedelic," Mike reflected. "I remember Fred getting shocked a couple times in the rain. People were holding the amps up because they were going to blow over."

With traffic sounds eliminated, Agape's roar carried on the wind, echoing off the concrete, providing thunder in the key of E. People camping or partying up and down the length of the Parade route were drawn to the parking lot.

The "ground-troops," of up to 300 witnesses from the Church in the Park, passed out Gospel tracts, engaging people in personal evangelism. With the crowd swelling into the street, Agape played through their one-hour set, "sharing Jesus" with a crowd that continued to grow past midnight.

When the concert was over, huddling in small groups under street lamps, the members of Agape prayed, read scripture and rejoiced with new converts until early in the morning. That part, the "afterglow," was the part they found most rewarding, the music just the vehicle to get them there.

With the crowd of sidewalk-campers slowly returning to their spots, and the Parade starting at 8am, viewers were filling the streets at 6am to lay claim to a good location. Somewhere between one and one and a half million people would watch the parade unfold.

On New Year's Day 1971, Reverend Billy Graham was the Grand Marshall in Pasadena's *Tournament of Roses Parade*. Beginning at the corner of Green Street and Orange Grove Blvd. the parade traveled north at a leisurely 2 1/2-miles per hour.

Among the 10s-of-thousands lining the Parade route, Billy Graham was greeted by hundreds of "Jesus Freaks," some of whom had filtered out from the Agape gathering ending only a few hours earlier.

Holding up placards reading "God is Love," they pointed their index fingers toward Heaven signifying, "One-way," a growing symbol of the Movement.

Something about that simple witness, at that moment in time, struck a profound chord with Billy Graham. It awoke something within him.

He later wrote, "Despite the fanfare, the flag-waving, I have seldom had such mixed emotions as I had that day in Pasadena. I watched the horizon for a cloud of impending revival to restore America's spiritual greatness.

Suddenly, we were made dramatically aware that a brand-new spiritual awakening was on its way."[2]

Coincidently, or prophetically, the theme for that year's parade was, "Through the eyes of a child."

David Wilkerson and, now, Billy Graham? With two of the most effective and respected Evangelists of the Twentieth Century finding common faith with the counter-culture converts, Evangelical Christianity would soon turn the same corner.

Six months later, in the early Summer of 1971, Agape had a very unproductive tour of Northern California and Oregon. With few more than 20 people showing up for their gigs, the ride home was depressing.

---

[2] Billy Graham, *The Jesus Generation*, Zondervan, 1971

John Peckhart sat staring out the window, his arms folded across his chest. The air, heavy with a shared discouragement, weighed everyone down. Without diverting his gaze from the passing mile markers, John informed his band mates, "I'm out." Uninterested in discussing the matter, his mind was made up.

Mike sighed, "We didn't know what to do next."

Other than the professional boost he provided for the music, John Peckhart's brief tenure with Agape was marked by one distinction: "John didn't give his testimony at gigs as was normally expected from us," Mike observed.

That's because John had a "carry-over" from his old life, something he and Ron discussed several times. While the details are now unimportant, Ron felt it disqualified John from representing Jesus.

Asking Fred if the band had any rules for when they were on the road, he responded, "No, not really. Except maybe, 'Don't sin.'"

Now searching for their third bass player in two years, an organic and elegant solution quickly presented itself. As with John Peckhart, Richard Greenburg was already part of the Fellowship, often assisting as one of the band's roadies.

Reminiscent of Fred with the White Klapp, Richard was another lead guitarist and song-writer, thrilled to plug into Agape's music ministry even if it meant playing bass.

With boatloads of skill and enthusiasm, the only thing he lacked was a Bass guitar and amp. Summoning the courage, Richard asked his mom for help. His mother, thrilled to learn Richard wanted to do something positive with his music and life, hooked him up with his dream rig.

If John Peckhart deepened and solidified the groove, Richard Greenburg widened it with melodic overtones and counter-synced rhythms.

"He was reeeally gcoooood," Fred remembered with some fondness. "I rever had to direct him. I just left him alone and he came up with some really good bass parts."

Referring to Richard's inflections and "licks," Mike remarked, "He was quite a crazy bass player."

While all of this was going on, Mike married former witnessing partner Sharron Bassett in September. "We were paying $155 a month in a rental house and going completely broke," Mike laughed "not even knowing how to make next month's rent. But we had a garage, and so, here comes the Boys. And within two weeks we had ten to 15 tunes dialed in, enough to go play."

Fully re-loaded, the new trio took off for a few concerts in Fresno. Christians there were very supportive of the band, opening their homes for the musicians and their entourage to stay.

Brushing his teeth in the morning, Mike "heard some guy blowing jazz on the piano in the other room. I walk in the room, toothpaste running out the corners of my mouth, to find Jim Hess. And I'm going, 'Dude!'"

Among the roadies who helped set up the gear, Jim was a young piano player who graduated High School the year after Fred and company.

Mike finished, "I'm watching Jim play and I thought, 'Holy smokes, where's this guy been?'"

Mike was blown away by something he never thought the band could use; a jazz-oriented pianist. As big a deal as adding a superior musician proved to be, Jim's skill on keys wouldn't be his biggest asset to Agape.

Possessed of a kind and gentle demeanor, Jim Hess would be an excellent counterpoint, the 'Peace Maker," to Fred and Mike's audacity; the "Storm Oil" of ancient mariners.

"So, the music changed a bunch," Mike noted. "There was a great deal of talent there and the dynamic really changed when Jim and Richard came. I just walked into the music and kind of went crazy with it."

Now fully armed, with a fully-formed sound, the newly constituted Agape began to move toward something beyond "three chords and an attitude."

Grinding out the now familiar trek up Highway 99, past Kingsburg, Fresno and "all these different, funny towns, mountain sort of towns," as Mike described them, "It was like a new revival in the band."

Turning the tables on their critics who complained, "You guys could raise the dead with that racket," they cranked it up one more decibel and hit the road with a renewed vision, a renewed joy.

Yet, in spite of all their adventures and thousands of miles already logged, our raucous lads remained one merit badge shy of their "official" *Road Warrior* status.

All they lacked was a great Road Story; something that would make a mother weep and other musicians laugh; something people would write about in their band bio. Not a Richie Valens, Big Bopper or Hank Williams kind of legend but, you know, something noteworthy.

With Thanksgiving fast approaching, Mike, Richard, Fred and Jim were about to take their test, earning that auspicious award in a powder-blue, Ford Econoline van.

John Peckhart, Fred Caban, Mike Jungman

Richard Greenburg

Jim Hess

Front Cover: Gospel Hard Rock, 1973

Back Cover: Gospel Hard Rock, 1973

The Band That Could
Raise the Dead

T raveling east out of the San Francisco Bay area on I-580, Agape and its entourage headed toward the final concert of a "short tour." It was Thanksgiving week, 1971, and every one of them looked forward to the respite from their non-stop schedule.

The Grand Theater on Central Avenue in Tracy, now known as *The Grand Theatre Center for the Arts*, was a perfect venue for the final gig. Seating close to 500, the crowd encouraged the band and the band responded.

Richard Greenburg remembered. "We were playing at their theater, like a movie theater, and it was going very well."

By Richard's modest standards, "very well" actually meant, great! This was one of those rare nights for a group of musicians when everything goes right; when the band is "tight;" when your fingers outpace your brain; when everything just flows, turning you into a joyful observer as much as a participant.

Richard continued, "And when we were playing, I felt the Holy Spirit and had a vision of Jesus using me like a puppet on strings to play my bass. I was serving Him and He was playing through me. I was feeling very close to the Lord and very anointed."

"The anointing" is a spiritual unguent God uses to grease our wheels and move us closer to Himself. It's what they all felt. Like professional athletes with nothing more to give, they left it all on the field.

Following their normal pattern of playing, praying and sharing scripture until midnight or later, band members finally loaded their gear for the trip home.

Stacking the instruments and amps in the cargo area at the rear of the van, they loaded the last piece, the Fender Rhodes piano, on top of the pile.

With 300 miles and a five-hour drive ahead of them, they hoped to be home by morning. But an unusual fog, rolling in from the Pacific, threatened their all-night trek.

Since Dashiell Hammett started writing *The Maltese Falcon* at a small table in *John's Grill* in San Francisco, the Bay area fog has been mythologized, romanticized and demonized:

"The fog in the night blurs the streets as Spade makes his way to an alley where a group of men are huddled."

With stories of easy vice and hard virtue, *Film Noir* found its American roots in San Francisco instead of Hollywood because of the phenomena. Though inland from the Bay, the route home was none-the-less inundated with cloud.

Richard Greenburg remembered. "I was driving my own car, a light-blue Dotson Wagon, and we were ahead of Ron in the van. It was extremely foggy, so foggy we could hardly see anything in front of us."

Heading south on the I-5 Freeway, Ron drove the donated, powder-blue van, Eila rode "shotgun" and the other, bone-weary pilgrims quickly nodded off to sleep. Mike reclined in the first row behind the Turners while Fred and Jim occupied the back area with the equipment.

About two hours into the trip, near State Route 152 at Los Baños, Californ a, "in the middle of nowhere," a carload of fools was ambling along ahead of them at 25 MPH on the darkened, fog-blanketed Interstate.

With their lights turned off.

Trying to imagine what the occupants of the vehicle were thinking, with the fog hanging like a death-shroud over their car, we can only conclude that, "they was havin' themselves a moment."

Though ahead of the van, Richard's car was in the other lane. "I might not have been able to see a car that I passed in the thick fog."

Ron didn't see them until it was too late.

"I was close enough to hear the crash and see Ron's headlights through the fog," Richard told me. "I pulled over and walked back to the accident."

"Ran up the back of these folks," Mike added.

The impact was sufficiently violent to invoke the laws of Force and Physics, propelling the 125-pound piano four feet through the air. Sailing over the top of Fred and Jim, it landed like a bomb on Mike.

"So, I'm lying on one of the seats," he told me, "and BANG!, out of nowhere, dead in my sleep, a piano hits me really hard. So, broken clavicle, broken ribs, dislocated shoulder and paralyzed stomach; it was rough.

In the chaos of pain and broken cars, I remember Fred leaning over from the back seat, grabbing the handles of the keyboard case, picking it up and throwing it out of the van.

I could barely breathe because it hurt so bad. Eila was injured pretty good. And the guys we hit were totally blasted, dancing around us, screaming,

'That's what ya get rock star! That's what ya get.'

They must have figured out we were musicians from the gear laying all over."

Speaking of The Roadside Circus, Fred added, "And the guys were drunk; I mean, they were quite a show. We saw them throw their booze bottle into the bushes and then they came over and started doing this dance because they were just, really drunk."

Mike recalled, "Ron, Fred and Richard were keeping them away from us, protecting us. So, we're laying out there on the dirt, next to the van and Freeway. It's a very desolate area, and I'm thinking, 'Wow, this is nuts.'"

Fred shared his memory of it.

"Somebody hit the windshield. I don't know who it was, but they had a bloody forehead or something. You could see that the windshield was cracked from where the forehead hit it.

So, I was throwing stuff. Mike was pinned in with the Rhodes piano, so I grabbed that and kind of got that off him. And then there were speakers that I had to get off of some other people, too."

After the Emergency Vehicles finally arrived, Mike and Eila were hospitalized in Los Baños. While two weeks in the hospital and 8 more to recover made for a very challenging Holiday season, Agape rested, regrouped and staked their claim to one of the greatest road stories in Christian Rock history!

While Churches in Boise and Fresno threw them out because of "the devil beats," activists in the streets began to test and then embrace them.

Playing at Valley College in San Fernando Valley during "Religious Emphasis Week," Agape drew a crowd of 400-500 people. Mingled in that group were members of *the Jewish Defense League*.

The Jewish Defense League was founded by Rabbi Meir Kahane in New York City in 1968, "to protect Jews from local manifestations of antisemitism." Real or imagined.

Mike observed that they were, "Quite active and quite angry back then, a big presence, especially in the Valley."

The problem was, the band had the biggest P.A. system in the area, often making them a target for the radicals who insisted on "equal time" for the public reading of their most recent manifesto. Such short-term aggression proved much easier than setting up your own gig, getting your own gear and drawing your own crowd.

Brandishing nunchucks they may have purchased for themselves at Christmas, the Jewish Defense League marched forward, demanding equal time on the band's PA system.

Describing the moment, Mike reported, "They were yelling, screaming, doing the nunchuck thing. You know, swinging them around and walking right up to us and I thought, 'here it comes.'"

As Fred and Jim assumed defensive postures behind whatever amps they could, and Mike was "looking for a way to run," Richard Greenburg stepped up to the mic.

"My name is Richard Greenburg and there are four generations of Rabbis in my family."

"And it got quiet," Mike said. "I'm sitting there, thinking, 'I'm going to get my butt kicked.' And all of a sudden, they all said, 'Oh, man, we're all on the same page.' And we're hugging. And I'm confused."

Interpreting the action as "the Holy Spirit putting the fire out," they stood for half an hour, commiserating, rejoicing. It didn't matter as long as it didn't include bleeding and screaming.

"We're both in the same bucket," Mike commented, "and we both love God. What an amazing way for God to say, 'These guys belong to me.'"

A few months later, Agape was invited by a Christian Biker group, recent converts from the Outlaw clubs, to perform at a park in Berkely on Halloween. "The crazies were out," as Mike put it.

Darn that PA system.

Reminded of the earlier incident, Mike commented, "And we're playing, giving our testimonies. And again, the largest PA in town. And a group called the *Black Student Union*, which became the Panthers, came up. And they're lit up, and angry, and going to take the mic away. And initially we resisted.

As they came forward, a group of 20 guys, maybe more, we again assumed a defensive posture. And then it got worse. The bikers rolled out and surrounded them and I thought, 'This is going to get ugly.' And once again, there's maybe 300 people watching this.

And right before it looked like the first blows were going to go, God's spirit just landed on everybody. And all of these black guys are saying, 'You know, I grew up in Church' and they're hugging me and Fred and everybody. The testimony of God brought that peace.

We were there till three in the morning praying with people. And all of a sudden, we were part of the Black Student Union. I mean, it was just amazing to watch God do that."

While maintaining an ongoing ministry, the band started work on their second album, *Victims of Tradition*. The addition of Richard Greenburg and Jim Hess made the music better so they really wanted everything to be better. It had to have a cool cover.

Riffing on the spiritualized notion of "the dead playing for the dead," it would be *seriously cool* to take the pictures in a graveyard, "among the tombs."

"Which one, how are we doing it?" wasn't their purview. That was Ron's job and it was something he was good at: making things happen.

Driving into Oak Park Cemetery in Montclair, to an elevated spot previously identified by Ron, the group of a dozen people worked in silence setting up enough equipment to create a realistic image of a live concert.

Overlooking acres of headstones, the black-and-white picture was taken from the back while they pretended to play for the Dead.

Mike described the photo shoot. "So, yeah, I mean, literally, we drove on, unpacked the gear and just acted like we were supposed to be there."

Fred mentioned, "You could see the workers were starting to talk to each other, trying to figure out what was going on. When they did chase us, we were already done."

Very cool cover? Check. It was time to hit the studio.

Recording at Buddy King Studios in Huntington Beach, the group wasn't under the pressure they'd felt recording the first album.

Buddy King was very familiar with the growing influence of the new Christian music, recording and producing many of the original tracks for the *Maranatha! Music* releases in 1970.

Recording artists like Brush Arbor, Bob Ayala, the Maranatha Singers and Children of the Day, Buddy turned his home into a "proper" recording studio, helping many of the earliest artists hone their craft.

Fred remembered, "So, this guy had like an average four-bedroom house and the whole thing had been turned into a 32-track studio.

He blocked off the dining room for a sound room, the studio, the playback room, and then everything else in the house apparently. Jim was down the hall in a bedroom with a piano.

And there was a lot of late-night work on the mix down, cutting pieces of tape back there. When I did the reverse guitar solo thing, you cut pieces of tape, put it inside out. Crazy, weird stuff. Anyway, so, yeah, that was about, maybe, four days going down there and doing that."

Recording only eight songs for the project, Jim, Richard, Mike and Fred poured it out, making every lick count. The quality of the final product repaid them for the effort.

"Awesome stuff. If the musicians who made this are still here, thank you for your amazing musicianship and creativity. You even give Larry Norman and Glass Harp something to aspire to. Yeah, I know Norman is dead and I wonder if he knew about you guys. This is a one-of-a-kind and a really good album." [online posting from Steven Goranson]

While the first album was released under Marlin Jones' *Mark Records*, this one, *Victims of Tradition* would be released under their own label: Renrut, Turner spelled backwards.

Simultaneous to the spiritual revival taking place, a musical revival broke out among many thousands of American musicians. Turning away from the limitations of "formula driven" music – simple, easily relatable "Pop" tunes one might observe on Dick Clark's Bandstand – it was a revolution of meter, method and meaning.

Bending the rules of song writing, every note and beat was being reviewed, reshaped, reimagined. Sound itself and the influence of aural space were being explored. It was a Rock 'n Roll Renaissance for musicians from then until now.

Between 1967 and 1973, creativity in popular music reached its apex. Along with Christian Rock, other sub categories of Rock 'n Roll fusions were being born with some regularity. It seemed that, no matter where you turned on the radio dial, magic was happening.

Labeled by William Shatner as "the Science Fiction of music,"[1] *Progressive Rock* featured contributions from Frank Zappa, YES!, Pink Floyd, the Beach Boys *Pet Sounds,* the Grateful Dead and the Beatles *Sergeant Pepper's.*

Building on the legacy of artists like Hank Williams, Johnny Cash and George Jones, *Country Rock* took root. Buffalo Springfield, Bob Dylan, the Birds and the Nitty Gritty Dirt Band helped provide a now legendary foundation.

Even *Heavy Metal* found its progenitors in people like Link Wray, the Kinks, Led Zeppelin and Cream.

Secular or sacred, the exploration of new frontiers always involves an element of risk. People were taking chances, exposing themselves in their art. Members of Agape started to "jam," live on stage, taking a chance, making it up as they went along. Kind of like their first gig on Huntington Beach. Only better.

---

[1] Q&A: William Shatner, Rolling Stone Magazine, Andy Green September 11, 2013

Playing at Pasadena City College, while Richard and Fred finished setting up their gear, Mike Jungman and Jim Hess took off on a spontaneous, 20-minute groove that rewarded them with stomping feet, clapping hands and a standing ovation.

Mike remembers, "Richard and Fred were much more creatively oriented, but Jim and I were, how to put it, more pocket players, if that makes any sense; groove oriented, more jazz oriented.

Jim was at the piano and he began to roll off something that I followed. And it opened up wide. Jim was doing everything from Jerry Lee Lewis, jumping around, banging on the keys, and we were just having fun. It just blew open. And when it was over, both of us were laughing."

While they remember their shared sorrows differently, they all remember the shared laughter exactly the same. The down-right hilarity, the joy of the moment, in which all of them continue to find solace, was the spiritual connection that carried them through common road arguments like who's "gonna ride shotgun" or who gets the best room.

Adding another layer of complexity, Mike and Jim went back to school. Mike enrolled at Citrus College to pursue a music degree, then Azusa Pacific for a degree in Biblical Literature, later enrolling at Fuller

Theological Seminary to pursue a Masters in Near-eastern studies.

Jim also had a love for language but, for him, English was sufficient. Wanting to be a writer and teacher, he attended San Antonio Community College.

For Mike, jumping back into the educational pool was a great big deal. "Dropping out" of high school because of a near-crippling problem with dyslexia, the learning disorder severely affected his relationship with education.

Lonnie's father, Warren Campbell, was a professor at Citrus College who took Mike "under his wing." Lonnie shared with me, "Mike somehow found his way into my father's college history class. He told my dad that he wanted to do well but couldn't read or understand. My dad then taught him; Mike studied his brains out and got a Master's Degree."

Discipleship makes demands on people. Up-all-night musicians, they had to manipulate moments to find study time while on their one-week road tours.

"Discipline is remembering what you want." [2]

"It was common for us to vacate during the day and go find a library and study," Mike said. "I have vivid memories of Jim drooling in his sleep, on his

---

[2] David Campbell

homework in the library, because we were playing all night, praying all night with people."

Weariness of the road aside, Christianity was proving good for every one of them, challenging them, growing them, lifting them.

With all of Agape's members now digging deep into their music, ministry and physical reserves, they continued with an unprecedented schedule of performances.

Though churches continued to ignore them, a number of groups began to sponsor them for open-air concerts. Observing a repeated pattern, concert after concert, Mike mentioned a gig in San Diego with an estimated crowd of "a thousand people," scattered over a hillside park.

"And the first rows, if there's rows in a park, the first group of people in front of us were all believers from some group that had us down there. Farther out from them, say 30, 50ft cut farther, it was all unbelievers, doing their thing.

We had people come up to us from the front saying, 'Brother, we love you guys, and we love what you're doing, but we just don't understand why you have to play that kind of music.'

And within minutes, somebody from the rear areas would stumble through the front, saying, "Wow, brother, that was so great. But do you always have to talk about Jesus, man?'

There was always that dichotomy of the Christians who couldn't stand the music and the unbelievers, who would say, 'Wow, man.'

As people were coming forward, accepting Jesus, we were being scolded for our loud music."

Mr. Chuck Girard, of *Love Song*, remembered Agape's performances. "We were a little shocked," he said, "surprised might be a better word, because we never heard anybody do that. And I thought, Wow!

We were criticized for just having drums in the Church and these guys are out there doing this kind of music for God. Their lyrics were bold and it was obvious they were trying to win people to the Lord.

There weren't a lot of bands in those days, so it was unusual to see a band that wasn't from Calvary Chapel. The bands at Calvary tended to lean toward music which was similar to what we were doing, background harmonies and softer songs, kind of soft rock.

So, to hear these guys out there, kind of just punching it, was unfamiliar territory at that time. Reminiscent of the early San Francisco sound in spots, they can be proud of their work."

The deeply appreciated spirit of comradery in his words were reciprocated by the members of Agape.

Mike observed, "When we ran into Love Song, which was the only band we ever ran into because there weren't any others, it was an immediate connection because they were catching heat, too.

It was love and deep respect for each other from a distance, an immediate bond. They were clearly, very talented guys, better musicians than us. But it kind of didn't matter if your reason for being there was to preach the Gospel."

Concert after concert, mile after mile, memories of individual performances became a blur. The band was ubiquitous. Starting with parks, schools, businesses – anyplace they could set up – Agape moved toward larger arenas where they might reach and influence more people.

Playing in the Field House of the University of Colorado at Boulder, a conservatively numbered crowd of 4,500 people responded to a week of advertising on local Christian Radio stations and those of the University.

Ron Turner shed light on the size of the crowd. "We shipped 100,000 half-sheet flyers and they distributed them everywhere around the university. They were on every telephone pole, every tree, everywhere."

Fred offered, "I remember looking out in the audience and the stage lights made it really hard for me to see. I could only see the front couple of rows. I knew there were a lot of people out there because I could hear them clapping, screaming and hollering."

Six years earlier, Fred Caban jumped into Billy Avelos' VW Bug looking for a moment exactly like this. Pursuing Jesus instead, here he stood in lights too bright to see. Now in possession of everything but the cash and bad reputation, Agape enjoyed the crowds, schedule and name recognition of the Rock stars they'd once wanted to be.

Grinning from ear to ear, Fred Caban stepped up to the microphone and yelled, "Hiiiiiii, we're Agape and we're here to play."

Muting the strings with his left hand, Fred treated his guitar like a percussion instrument, beating out an impromptu groove:

> Thump, chiky chik, chiky chick, chiky chik chik,
> Thump, chiky chik, chiky chick, chiky chik chik.

And, on the ensuing downbeat, a crowd of Boulder's finest was introduced to the music and ministry of Agape.

"We played wide open," Mike remembered joyfully.

"We just start jamming," Fred offered. "After we got done, everyone applauded, cheered and whistled and then we started doing our songs."

For one hour, the crowd in the Field House tapped their toes, "bobbed" their heads and found themselves moved by an approach to the Good News they'd never before experienced.

By the time the band was done, without a sermon, an altar call or an officially religious closing prayer, people began "clamoring," was the oft-used word, to approach the stage.

"They were crazy and openly wanting to know about Jesus," Mike said. "I almost ran over my kit to get off stage and meet folks. We were up all night, talking and praying with folks. There weren't enough of us to reach all the people that wanted to hear more."

What a wonderful dilemma.

July, 1974, marked the zenith for the combined ministries of Agape and Ron Turner. Doing slight violence to Charles Dickens, "It was the best of times, it was the epoch of belief, it was the season of light." [3]

Having planted two more congregations, one in Saugus Park and the other in Salt Lake City, Ron was extended an invitation to be a member of the *First*

_____

[3] "A Tale of Two Cities," Charles Dickens, 1859

Congress of World Evangelization sponsored by Billy Graham in Lausanne, Switzerland.

Receiving the invitation via the recommendation of Azusa Pacific's Dr. Haggard, Ron was a Seminar speaker "sharing about our Ministry," he said.

"Hearing great teaching, 12 hours a day-and-night, from various Evangelists chosen from around the world," Ron joined with 2,700 Evangelical leaders from 150 countries.

Back home in Covina Park, the entire Fellowship found great joy amid a growing sense of legitimacy garnered from Ron's blessing. People all over the world now knew about their church, about them; a powerful and unanticipated reward for such young visionaries.

Flying home from Switzerland, Ron and Eila landed at LAX in the middle of the night. On the plane with them was well-known, Southern Gospel composer and performer, Bill Gaither.

Waiting for Ron and Eila were about 200 of the Covina Park Fellowship. Lining the hall at the airport, they sang praise songs and lifted a large banner that read, "Welcome Home Rev." Every face was lit up.

"Crazy love," is what Ron fondly remembered.

Bill Gaither thought all of it was for him; he stuck his arms up in the air to wave to everyone. He figured it out.

By the end of the long summer of 1974, Larry Eskridge estimated that the Jesus Movement saw at least 250,000 people become Christians.

But the revival was coming to a close.

While religious activity continued unabated, the innocence, liberty and hunger – the "anguish for souls," – as described by David Wilkerson, was fading away.

Summer was ending, autumn was upon them and long shadows would soon begin to fall in Covina Park.

A few months after their grand accomplishments, after such a powerful, positive and emotional year, the violated quote of Charles Dickens was about to be made whole:

"It was the age of foolishness, it was the epoch of incredulity, it was the winter of despair."

Unaccustomed to dancing on shifting carpets, the members of Agape and their closest friends were about to have the rug pulled from under them.

Front Cover: Victims of Tradition, 1972

Back Cover: Victims of Tradition, 1972

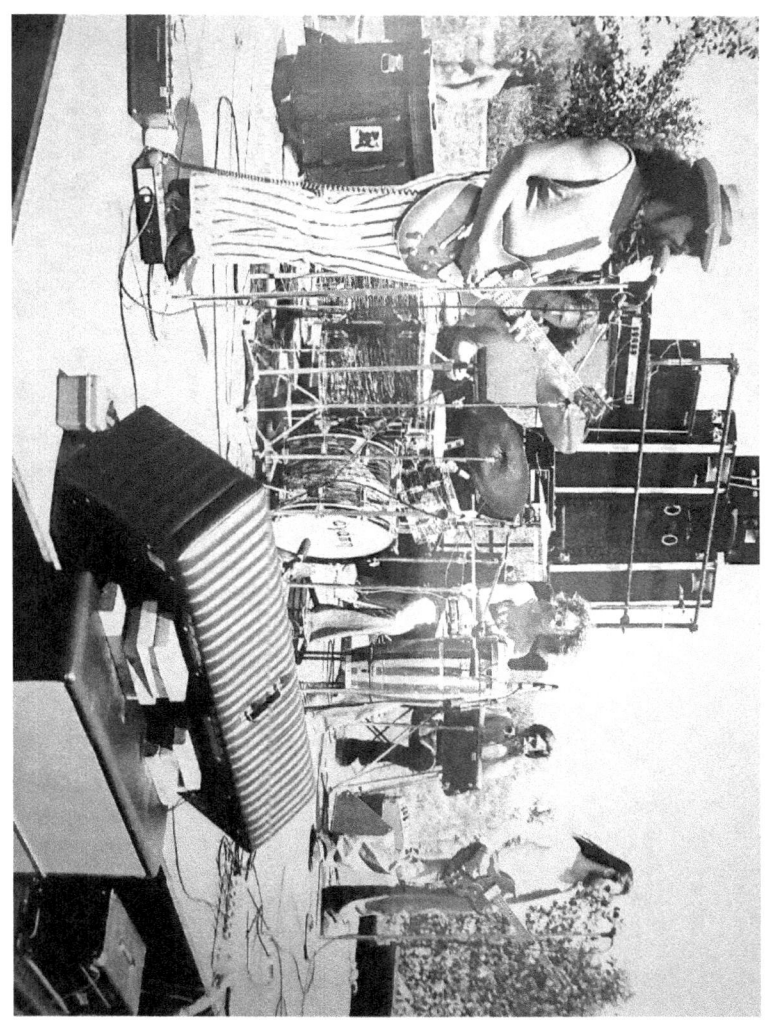

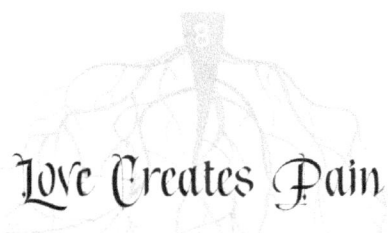

Love Creates Pain

Generally speaking, storytelling has a preference for "happily-ever-after," such endings often the result of fortuitous circumstance or unusual displays of grit. When a delightful conclusion proves elusive, one may be manufactured by an author's strategic choice about where to stop writing.

With that in mind, this tale should have stopped at the end of the last chapter. But that's called revisionism and it looks for a happy ending in the wrong place. As long as no one looks behind the curtain, revisionism can ignore painful moments, creating an illusion of serendipity.

However well-intended such a literary approach may be, integrity is inevitably lost and what might have been a true story of God's grace becomes nothing more than historical fiction.

Commenting on historical revisions of the Jesus Movement in the 2023 film, *The Jesus Revolution*,[1] Lonnie Frisbee's wife, Connie said,

"The truth is that dealing with people is very messy. And they want to make it very tidy. They've tidied it all up so much that it just stinks to high heaven. That's not how it was.

If the truth were known, I wouldn't look so good. Lonnie wouldn't look great. Chuck Smith wouldn't look good. Greg Laurie wouldn't look good.

But who would look good? God would be looking stellar."[2]

Wrestling with angels over the possibility of leaving a blemish on the legacy of Agape or the cause of Christ, the "Agape fiasco," as it was called, would not be included here, at all, if it weren't the ax laid to the root of their story.

Looking for the redemptive threads lining the frayed edges of their memories, I found solace in the writings of Scottish evangelist and Christian thinker, Oswald Chambers. "The Bible does not idealize its characters but allows us to see the seamy-side of the tapestry

---

[1] "The Jesus Revolution," Lionsgate films, February 24, 2023.

[2] "Connie Frisbee's surprising reaction to 'Jesus Revolution' movie," *God Reports,* Mark Ellis, March 13, 2023. With permission.

that we might better recognize the grace that so freely forgives." [3]

Sometime in mid-November,1974, band members became aware of two Sisters from the Covina Park fellowship who accused Ron of an insult to their honor. Reported as a crime of words and a violation of personal space, Ron later acknowledged his conversations and body language to have been incredibly "immature."

Saved about the same time as Fred and Mike, band members knew the women before they knew Ron; they had a history together. Preaching from the back of a truck in fast-food parking lots, kneeling in the gravel of the outdoor theaters and witnessing to outcasts on the street, the women were battle-hardened "brethren."

While the pair had certainly been exposed to many inappropriate and "creepy" suggestions from men before, this wasn't just "a guy." This was their Pastor, the man of God they'd watched lead thousands to Christ.

How do they process this? Do they tell their husbands? Would *anyone* believe them? Could they ignore it, pretend it never happened? Is that what Jesus required of women?

---

[3] Oswald Chambers, "My Utmost for His Highest," 1924.

Reported as "overwhelmed with disgust," when listening to Ron talk about relationships, and afraid to be anywhere near him, the women would have left the church had their husbands not been involved in positions of leadership.

They felt trapped.

Attempting to follow the admonition of Scripture, counsel was sought from one of the "elders," one of the more experienced women of the church. Torn in many directions, the tempest awakened within them required resolution.

The goal of mature Christian women teaching the younger was, "so that no one will malign the word of God." [4] Already too late for that, the seekers were further devastated by another violation of their trust.

After sharing the ugly details of the offense, after pouring out their souls, they were advised,

"Do you remember what happened to Miriam when she spoke against Moses? God struck her with leprosy. Don't *ever* say anything about God's anointed because they're protecting Christ."

Protecting Jesus from the reputation of preachers is a futile business. Our Christian penchant for sweeping

---

[4] Titus 2:3-5

"inconvenient" things – things like wounded people – under the rug has *never* benefitted the cause of Christ.

What a mess. Now what?

Deeply troubled, Mike arranged a meeting with Ron to figure out what was going on. Accompanied by his wife, Mike and Sharron talked with Ron and Eila in their home. It didn't go well. For anyone.

Reflecting on the moment, Mike emphasized, "'RUN!' is what God told me."

Describing the aftermath in the weeks that followed, Mike explained, "We were publicly excommunicated. People we loved were warned against us and told to have nothing to do with us."

Sharron added, "Mike and I actually received hate mail from a member in the church stating we were of the devil."

Ron Turner remembered things differently. "Mike talked to me on a Wednesday night. They were just gone. There was never an announcement that they left."

With no interest in picking at dark spots, innocence or guilt, heroes or villains are not for me to determine. But when you're writing about the memories of living people, all of whom have access to attorneys, you're wise to seek clarification from credible sources.

Daniel Vraa was a 19-year-old student attending Mount San Antonio College when he saw a group of "long haired hippie freaks" sitting in a circle. They were having an open-air Bible study. Curious, he sat down and said, "This is what I'm looking for. Who are you guys?"

Learning they were from the Agape Fellowship, he started attending Wednesday night Bible studies and then Sunday morning services. Daniel's experiences were typical of the 350 - 500 energized people who regularly attended the Agape Covina Park Church.

Selected by Ron to be one of the leaders of the Future Ministers, Daniel was eventually viewed by the diaspora of Covina Park as "the unofficial pastor for the remnants of the ministry."

Earning a Master of Divinity degree from Fuller Theological Seminary in 1981, Daniel was ordained in the Presbyterian Church in 1982, eventually serving as Senior pastor at the Dixon, California, Community Church for many years.

The definition of a good man, it was clear he loved Ron Turner. It was also clear that he represented the feelings of many other eyewitnesses to the sad unfolding of events.

"In two years, Ron not only taught me the Bible but he taught me *how* to study and learn the Bible and it became the centerpiece of my ministry the whole time I was a pastor," Daniel commented.

"Ron was raised in a family of dysfunctional alcoholics. He grew up a deeply wounded man who was doing the best he knew how. He was one of the most lovable people on Earth and I truly believe it was genuine, not a put on."

Asking specifically if Mike, Sharron and the other ostracized believers were treated as brethren who had erred or as enemies of the cross of Christ, Daniel caught his breath and paused.

"First of all, we were all heartbroken and stunned. It was like a divorce because we really were a family. For me, and the people I hung with, we were all stunned and hurt. And at first it was like, 'How could they do that?'

The family was breaking up, the church, and I didn't want our Pastor to run down these people. I loved Mike. It's like, I want a little explanation, then move on. I guess he felt so threatened by their leaving, their position on things and what they said. I don't know.

I can't remember anything specifically he said, but I just remember it, generally. He would speak to it and, I mean, he'd take his time. And what's interesting, the more he talked, the less people sided with him," Daniel observed.

"It's like listening to somebody and thinking, 'Wait a minute, that's not the guy I know.'

Something's wrong here.

And yet we don't want to lose what God is doing here, and we don't want to dishonor God.

When I first met him, he was like the Apostle Paul to me. My first three years with him were Heaven on Earth. The last two were like the King Saul story.

If you talk to him, tell him I still love him."

Two weeks after Mike's departure, contemplating what he should do, Fred attended a Future Minister's meeting. "I wasn't one of them but I liked to stop in once in a while to keep up with what was going on."

Parking his car and walking across the lot, Fred was approached by Ron who wanted a private conversation with him before entering the building.

"There's a lot going on around here, Fred, and I need to know if you're with me or not."

According to multiple reports, one of the first things to happen after Ron's meeting with Mike involved the distribution of a contract, a "Loyalty Pledge," that everyone jokingly referred to as "Ze Papers." As in, "You vil zign ze Papers."

Sign it or you're out! That was the gist of it. At least, what they remember of it. A long time coming, Fred

Caban opted for "out." His stubborn independence, and what he saw as Ron's new, authoritarian style, could no longer co-exist.

"Well, yeah." Fred began. "I support you but I go to God directly. I don t go to you. Martin Luther didn't do what he did for us that we might be standing here talking about submission to a man. I have a direct relationship with God. And whatever *He* says, I do."

"And then," Fred reported, "Ron said, 'Well, then, I don't want you here.' And that was it."

Ron's memory of it was different. Briefly conjecturing about anything that might have been misinterpreted as a loyalty pledge. he finally declared, "There was no document."

Ultimately, the discrepancies, the "he said, she said," don't matter to our story. The devil is, indeed, in the details.

In the end, the schism wasn't so much about the Box of Monsters the women opened or "Ze paper" Fred refused to sign. The separation of souls was more about the person Ron had allowed himself to become.

"Love (ἀγάπη/Agape) is never tired of waiting. Love is kind, knowing neither jealousy nor envy. Love is neither forward nor self-assertive; boastful or conceited. Love doesn't keep a list of wrongs or behave itself in a provocative manner. Love isn't happy about bad news but rejoices with the truth."

In that brief moment of time, completely out of character with the whole of his life, all of that now seemed gone from the man.

"I wasn't in the room when any of that happened. But I just wish Ron wouldn't have gone into it so much. And I guess that's what kind of turned me away." Daniel lamented.

The way we treat each other, when we meet each other at the bottom, says much about the truth of things.

For six years, the strained partnership found great success because everyone was committed to the same goal. For the cause of the Kingdom, everyone was willing to make sacrifice and concession. As long as there is satisfaction, people will sacrifice. When satisfaction leaves, sacrifice will soon follow.

The iron was no longer sharpening iron. The friction from that exercise now served only to ignite the spark that burned down the world they'd so prayerfully constructed.

Too often, in the Church of Flawed People, *Love Creates Pain*.

Though 95% of the Church in the Park continued forward undeterred, for the members of Agape and those closest to them, the last straws fell exceedingly heavy. For one reason or another, whether Ron remembered it or not, they all felt betrayed.

Interestingly, Ron Turner felt the same way.

There was no getting past this. With their long-eroding trust now irreparable, the die was cast and the partnership of Agape was over.

Attempting to understand the truth of things, I reached out to Ron via email, social media and phone messages. I was excited when, after many months, I answered the phone to hear,

"Hello, Joe? This is Cowboy Ron,' Ron Turner returning your calls. Thanks for your persistence."

Eventually migrating to Montana with Eila to be near their daughter, the two of them opened a business, *The Cowboy Cabin*. Offering a truly amazing inventory of "Old-west" antiques and collectables, the smell of homemade bread baking in the store's old, wood stove helped set the stage for a "sentimental journey West."

His head over-flowing with knowledge, experience and opinion, Ron spoke for most of 25 minutes. The first our many conversations, it proved insightful.

Basically, a getting-to-know-you call, he offered one bit of unsolicited insight. While my questions were about the beginnings of their work and challenges of their journey, he unexpectedly interjected,

"I didn't *lose* my church, by the way; just so you know. It was taken from me."

A half-century of memories, settling like layers of sediment in shale, revealed that much woundedness yet remained in those closest to the story. Especially for the offender and offended.

Reflecting on all of it, Ron stated, "I have learned from so many things, including my own errors, to be more sensitive; to minister and not allow myself to be swallowed up with a lot of garbage."

Ron Turner was a good man. There is no doubt of that. Committing much to help the band realize their desires, he and Eila inspired many to better themselves and become a blessing to their world. There is much, much to be admired.

But, like all of us, he also made some bad choices and hurt some folks along the way. There is, also, no doubt of that.

While there are long trails of Jesus Movement success stories – churches spawned, multitudes of converts registered and good deeds done – there is no punch line for the collateral damage in a spiritual war.

By the close of 1974, the Jesus Movement had been commercialized and incorporated into the American culture. Paraphrasing *the Doobie Brothers*, "Jesus was just alright" with just about everybody. Though people were already lining up to take credit for God's movement, the glory, innocence and power of it all was disappearing.

Then again, maybe everybody just got older, more jaded, less inclined to believe in miracles. Especially in their own lives. Maybe Peter Pan simply grew up and could no longer see, "Through the eyes of a child."

The Church in the Park and Agape now became two, separate entities. As far as Fred and Mike were concerned, they were a band before Ron came along and there was no reason that should change now. Jim Hess and Richard Greenburg agreed.

They only had one more performance scheduled, one last commitment to honor. Confounding any sense of irony, the date was Friday, the 13th of December, at Mount San Antonio College. If needing a date filled with symbolism and consequence, Friday the 13th would suffice.

After that, they were on their own.

Voyaging Pilgrims

December 13th came and went. The second most memorable concert in Agape's history and none of the participants had any clear memory of the details. An awkward moment for all, every performance up to this day had been a cheery, "Hello! Welcome to God's Kingdom."

Unfamiliar with tragic goodbyes, the dynamic was completely changed. Feeling strangely of "tinkling cymbals and sounding brass," the performance reflected a lyric from Elinore Rigby: *"No one was saved."* That had never happened before.

Richard Greenburg offered, "When we fired Ron as our manager, we fired him as our evangelist too. We put on one last concert and this time he was asked not to preach and there was no altar call. But Ron graciously took part. He stood up at the end and asked the audience to shout for an encore."

"It was hard," Fred told me. "We were playing for people we knew more than having an evangelical outreach type of thing."

Mike added, "And it was becoming clear that we didn't want to let go of stuff but, we knew. It was hugs and prayer. Lovely, on the best part of us.

We also knew we were dependent on the Lord. We knew where our hearts needed to be anchored."

Though, "under new management," band members had no reason to believe there wasn't a future for their music. Converting an old goat barn south of Azusa into their own studio and rehearsal space, the four musicians grew tighter, smoother, better.

His own, worst critic, Mike Jungman observed, "The music was the best it had ever been."

The influence of Jim Hess and Richard Greenburg finally allowed Agape to realize the full potential of "their own sound." The holy grail for any band, it requires every musician to surrender their own musical preference to achieve it. They, and their music, were finally growing up.

But, after months of intense rehearsals, they couldn't get any gigs. Two albums, hundreds of venues played, thousands of miles travelled, more professional than they'd even been, and they began to slowly realize that their moment might have passed.

Richard Greenburg kept things going with a solo project he called, "The Rapid Richard Project." Writing the music while Agape was still active, Fred, Mike and Jim all contributed to the tracks.

"I'd be at our little goat shed recording my music and we'd still be practicing there. And I was trying to put together an album. Agape hadn't yet been disbanded and they were helping me out."

But, for the pioneering band of Agape, it was just the last glimmer of light before the darkness descends.

The Soundtrack of the Jesus Movement had cataloged its final entries and the emerging genre of Contemporary Christian Music had no place for bands that "sound like the world." The experimentation was over.

Born of innocence and spiritual liberty, the outside-the-box kind of thinking that launched the new Christian music seems to have disappeared when calling became vocation.

As Chuck Girard lamented, "It became more about entertaining the troops than it was about winning the war."

Commercialization civilized Christian Rock.

In 1971, Calvary Chapel stopped using Buddy King for their recordings and launched *Maranatha! Music.* By now, 1974, Calvary was home-base for more than a dozen music groups.

Popularizing a folk-rock style, this *Second Wave* of musicians included groups like the Sweet Comfort Band, Children of the Day, The Way, Debby Kerner, Mustard Seed Faith, Karen Lafferty and Daniel Amos.

In 1972, Billy Ray Hearn, a graduate of Baylor University with a degree in Church Music, started Myrrh Records signing folks like Barry McGuire, Randy Matthews and Nancy Honeytree.

Composer Ralph Carmichael formed Light Records and, by 1974, had signed Andrae Crouch and the Disciples, the Archers, the Winans and both Tramaine and Walter Hawkins.

By now, Kurt Keiser and Word Records had risen to the top of the new industry. Signing artists like Amy Grant, Michael W. Smith, Rich Mullins, Russ Taff and the Imperials, the artists helped establish the pattern for what the new "Christian Rock" music would sound like.

Nowhere, in the entire universe of the newly created genre, was there any room for groups like Agape.

Perhaps they simply weren't good enough. Perhaps they weren't polished enough or malleable enough. Perhaps, their inability to "be all things to all men," and do something other than "Gospel Hard Rock," closed their own door.

Whatever the reason, they'd been weighed in the balance of progress and found wanting. Agape was never going to square with the slick, suburban profile now evinced by CCM. Neither good nor bad, the work of devils or angels, it's just the way things turned out.

Fred observed, "We all realized that, somehow, all of this was coming to an end. People were talking about this 'worship thing' that was coming in. And we talked about it like, 'What is this thing? What does it mean to us?' We didn't understand it at the time but we kept hearing about it; that people are doing worship music now."

Equally discouraged by the past, present and future, "We decided to shut it down," he said.

Had they not outgrown the joyful naiveté of their beginnings, had their joy not been sufficiently eroded along the way, they might have toughed it out and found a home on the fringes of CCM. But not likely.

With their community gone, their ministry rejected and their Glendoran dream dissolved into sorrow, time quickly caught up with all of them.

Now in their mid-twenties, with families and grown-up responsibilities of their own, it was time to move on. But that wasn't going to be as easy as it sounded.

They weren't prepared for life in the real world. Not really.

By his own admission, Fred Caban "did not have a career path" outside of music.

"I was always doing some kind of funky job," he mentioned, "just doing stupid things. I worked for the newspaper in the press area and for years with a fencing company. Whatever was available."

Seeking a degree in music, Fred enrolled at Citrus College, Pasadena City College and Northridge College where he studied the creation of music with mainframe computers.

Following a road trip with some friends in September, 1975, Fred asked his girlfriend of several years, Lesa Caldarella, to marry him.

Fred met Lesa at a High School play featuring some of their mutual friends from the Covina Church. Having written two volumes of poetry before they met, Lesa impressed him with their shared love for words.

"He was a rock star in the Church," she told me. "Just somebody who loved God, loved his Bible, loved music and always had this kind of quirky sense of humor."

Meeting him after the release of Agape's first album, Lesa Caldarella became much more than Fred's muse. She became the best friend he would ever have.

"I feel like God has called me to marry you," Fred told her. "I don't want to live my life without you."

"And he wanted to do it right now," Lesa mentioned.

"Let's just go," Fred urged. "Let's just go to Vegas or something. Just get married."

"So off we went to Vegas," Lesa laughed.

Upon returning, their old friends rented a small room to celebrate.

"Sharron Jungman, Chere Hess and some of the people from the band, the wives or girlfriends, they had this little wedding cake for us. I had flowers in my hair and all that stuff."

Eventually, Lesa and Fred found great opportunities to work for World Vision. Founded in 1950 as an organization to provide emergency aid to Missionaries, *World Vision International* has become one of the world's most prominent Christian humanitarian aid and advocacy organizations.

Opening their small, rented house for Bible studies, Fred and Lesa did what we all do, they carved out a life.

After Agape's dissolution, Mike Jungman sought opportunities to play drums for contemporary Christian artists like Bob Ayala and several others.

Feeling like he'd been stereotyped as a power-blues drummer, he met disappointment at every turn.

"After Agape, I couldn't find anything. I auditioned with a couple of people I knew and nothing worked. Things finally got to where I sold everything. I ended up with a cello and a bad guitar. God had to finally take me out of music."

After ten years of pondering and wandering, Mike and Sharron attended a Sunday service at the Pasadena Four Square Church. The Associate Pastor, Chief Musician and Staff Evangelist was a former British rocker named Caleb Quaye.

Best known for his work in the 1960s and 70s with Elton John, Mick Jagger, Pete Townshend and Paul McCartney, Caleb turned it all over to Christ after his conversion in 1982.

Following a Sunday Service, Mike was introduced to Caleb who was made aware of his skills by a mutual friend at the church.

"So," Caleb started, "they tell me you play drums."

Thinking instantly of Jeff Newman on the campus of Azusa High School, Mike and Sharron felt comfortable enough to stay for three years. Better than that, after two weeks, Mike was "on the kit," playing worship services for the first time in his life.

After leaving the Covina Fellowship, Lonnie found her way into something that provided a new mission field: she became a music teacher. Starting with Glendora Unified, she also served in the Los Angeles Unified School District and 20 years in Garden Grove.

Thoroughly invested in private Christian schooling, Lonnie found joy in reporting that none of her children or grandchildren had attended Public Schools.

Working through the *Grace Evangelistic Ministries*, she preached the Gospel in 22 countries. "A lot of them were underground evangelism," she mentioned. "In countries where they don't let you preach the Gospel."

Taking lessons from Ron Turner and countless other evangelistic juggernauts, such things would never deter Lonnie Campbell Bissell.

Following a conversation with Ron about the role of Judas in a Passion Play, Richard Greenburg left the fellowship one year after Fred and Mike. The Play included hundreds of people, horses, realistic military garb, buildings, a marketplace and full musical score. Birthed by what Ron described as a vision when returning from Lausanne, the full production was worthy of its own TV Special.

Encouraging Richard to play the role, Ron told him, "You fit the part." Referring to his theatrical chops, Richard instead took it like a dagger to the heart.

Against the backdrop of everything that happened with his friends, and the tone of Ron's voice, Richard took the words personally, hearing them as a double-entendre. Being identified with Judas was too much.

Listening to Chuck Smith on Sunday morning TV, giving much time to prayer and reflection, he also made several attempts to make a success of his music.

"I tried to put together another group," he wrote me. "But, after a year, the Lord kept impressing on me to stop pursuing a career in commercial rock music."

At the Vineyard Church in Newport Beach, Richard met Jill Austin and worked as a piano player in her ministry, "Master Potter" for the next, four years.

Reflecting on his musical journey, Richard summed it up by saying, "I found worship and worship-leading were what God had designed my musical talent for." Strange confessions for a hard-core Christian rocker. Keeping pace with advancing technologies, Richard eventually took his ministry to the Internet. [1]

Like the others, Jeff Newman left the church with his faith and confidence shaken.

Traveling as Lead Guitarist with Thurlow Spurr and Larnell Harris, Jeff disconnected from an intimate walk

---

[1] https://richardgreenburg.com and https://sharefaith.site

with God and "at that point in my life, I was backsliding. I became a 'Church guy.'"

Going through the motions, spiritually wandering for several years, Jeff Newman fell in love and surrendered his sovereignty.

"All of a sudden, I realized that 'If I'm going to have any future with this woman, I've got to get right with you, Lord.' And so, I'm in the car all night long, all the way to Washington, DC, I'm repenting, asking God to forgive me for the last couple of years.

And sure enough, man, He says, 'Yeah, okay, son.' He welcomes me. And, you know how the Father is, right?

But He also said, 'Jeff, you need to lay your music down.

You just need to get rid of it all and don't play anymore, because that's a stumbling block. I want you out of the band and I want you in Louisville, Kentucky. I don't want you to go back. Don't go back to L.A.

I'm going to *change your calling in life.'"

Changing his calling meant that God was going to change Jeff. It would take some time and serious polishing.

Finding his first clue in Louisville, with his life-partner now joined to his journey, Jeff "picked up the scent" and followed a long, circuitous trail to Austin, Texas.

Beginning with Bible Studies in their home Living Room, Jeff and his wife established the Austin Vineyard Church in 1986, serving as Senior Pastor for 30 years before his retirement.

Characteristically modest, Jeff said, "So I ended up becoming a pastor. That's the short of it. I ended up becoming a Pastor."

Now a long way from the self-centered, arrogant, Rock-star guitarist of his youth, Jeff Newman finally fulfilled the vision planted in his spirit at the beginning of his journey. More than that, he lived out the dreams of all the zealous hopefuls gathered in Covina Park.

Following the departures of Fred, Mike and many of their earliest friends, Jim and Chere Hess struggled with what to do. Should they maintain their loyalties with their departed friends or should they continue to stand with their "maligned" Pastor and disintegrating church group?

Jim first met Chere Gladney in his Junior year of High School while working at the *Betsy Ross Ice Cream Shoppe* on Holt Avenue in Pomona. Chere was a Waitress and Jim was the "Scooper," smiling at her from behind the counter. Becoming "best friends," the two started dating a year later when Chere attended the Covina Park services.

In spite of the band's influence in their lives, Jim and Chere's investment had been in the Kingdom and they would stay until God directed them to leave.

Jim worked nights, cleaning at the Pomona Hospital. Seeking to serve without killing during the Viet Nam War, he enlisted in the Air National Guard, working out of March Air Force Base in Riverside, about an hour's drive southeast of Azusa.

The breakup of the band was particularly hard for him. Choking back the emotion, Chere explained, "It was kind of like his demise. It was really hard for him not to be a part of that because he loved those guys so much and he loved the music so much."

Feeling the same void as Fred, Mike and Richard, Jim continued to deal with the significant depression caused by the loss of his own dream.

Adding to the oppressive sadness, his life-long allergies were starting to get out of control. "He was spraying an antiseptic in his mouth all the time to numb his throat," Chere noticed.

Particularly annoyed by walnuts, Jim was living in the wrong corner of the world.

One of the most iconic trees in Southern California, the *Juglans californica,* is commonly known as the Southern California black walnut. It's everywhere. As trees go, it's small, could even be described as a large shrub. But, if you had the kind of allergies that troubled Jim Hess, they were more like Sequoias.

"They must know we're gonna play here and plant walnut trees on purpose," Jim often joked with the band. It's good he wasn't interested in being the vocalist.

After a few months of particularly problematic rawness in his throat, Jim asked Chere, "Could you take a look at the back of my mouth?"

Looking down his throat, Chere caught her breath.

"It was like this huge, watery, white-gum stuck behind his tonsil. 'Oh, my God, Jim, you got to get to the doctor and see this. I don't know what it is.'"

Failing to connect the dots Jim asked, "Can you just reach in there and take it out?"

Unable to wrap her mind around the size of the growth, Chere's speech stumbled.

"NO! I can't. It's just too big."

Arranging a doctor's appointment at Pomona Hospital for the next day, they then followed recommendations to take Jim to the hospital at the Stanford Cancer Center. After waiting two more, agonizing days for a diagnosis, the bottom fell away from their world, leaving them both concussed.

Though it had shown its face less than 30 times in history, Science was able to identified the flesh-eating monster living in Jim's throat. Its name was *Histiocytic Lymphoma*.

Rare, violent and extremely aggressive, the malignancy hid itself in Jim's body by mimicking the symptoms of his life-long allergies.

Oncologists offered them two options, both of which were nightmares.

The first would involve the removal of the right half of his face: down through his nose, his larynx, half his tongue, jaw and everything connected to the cancer.

Or, they could implant radioactive "BBs" around his tonsils and lymph nodes to see if that might reduce the swelling. No one was using the word, "cure" and their second idea sounded more like experiment than relief.

Married just two and a half years, and leaning hard on Jesus, Jim and Chere's collective breath was sucked away.

Recovering themselves, the couple asked if there were any other options. The twin monsters of chemo and radiation were the only things suggested.

Desperation can move people to do some surprising things. Christian or not, it doesn't matter. "All that a man has, will he give for his flesh."[2]

Just across the border in Mexico, cancer patients from around the world travelled to clinics offering injections of Laetrile, also called Vitamin B-17. A serum, made from apricot pits and other seeds, it was illegal as a cancer treatment in the United States.

But one of Jim's family members "knew some people who knew some people" and a meeting was arranged south of San Diego near the Mexican border.

Returning home with the vile of serum, Chere couldn't bring herself to administer the injections. Convinced she was only adding to his pain, she looked toward two sisters from the Agape Fellowship for help. Both Registered Nurses, their love for Jim and Chere moved them to break the law and jeopardize their own careers.

"They would come over in the morning and afternoon to give him a shot," Chere remembered. "The shots did nothing for him."

Combining the radiation and chemotherapy treatments at Stanford with the daily injections of

---

[2] Job 2:4 KJV

Laetrile smuggled n from Mexico, the prognosis remained grim. They were running out of options.

Hope is dependent upon options. Faith is not. As long as there are options, we can remain hopeful. When the options run out, faith is all that remains.

For Jim and Chere Hess, hope was now hanging by its last, slender thread.

Oncologists at Stanford told Chere, "If you can get Jim to the Mayo Clinic in New York, then he's got a chance. They remove the patient's blood, treat it with new antibiotics, create a serum and then put that back into his body to fight the cancer."

Mayo Clinic? New York? How in the world would they be able to make that happen?

Jim's mom had a distant, barely-known cousin living on Long Island. Reaching out to her in desperation, the family sheltered Jim and Chere for three weeks, Chere driving Jim to the hospital in Queens, twice a week.

Waking one morning, just prior to the end of the 3-week treatment, edema had inflated Jim's face, hands and feet, swelling until they appeared deformed.

After traveling back to the Mayo Clinic, Jim wasn't with the doctors very long before they brought him out in a wheelchair. The options had run out.

They told Chere, "You need to get home *now*. Fly him home *now*, because he's not going to last through the night."

Booking a Medical Emergency flight out of JFK, they travelled through the long, dark hours.

Weeping, Chere stammered, "People said, 'He was a monster. He looked terrible.' When we got back to the airport, Jim's mom, sister and uncles were there. They took him to the Pomona Valley Hospital. Jim and I were both born there."

After checking him in, something bordering on the miraculous occurred.

"God gave us a miracle," Chere told me. "Jim lived through the night and was like his old self. It was a miracle! They were going to do a tracheotomy but, there he was, perfect."

Fully embracing the belief that the avalanche of prayers had prevailed, that God had intervened and worked a miracle for all of them, Chere thought, "Oh, my God, he's going to live. He got healed! So, we took him home. I was taking care of him during the day and Jim's Mom took care of him all night."

The sudden jolt of resurrected hope coursed through the family like a double-shot of adrenaline.

Jim's family had already lost four of his siblings, his brother, Dave, within the last year. His mother, in fear of losing her last son, "Couldn't get over it," Chere reflected. "She was a wreck and threw everything she had into taking care of Jim."

But the moment of glory didn't last. "He was so thin. I could see it growing. It was horrible."

The despair returned. This time, neither Science nor Faith could lift the weight. Finally grown weary of the fight, the pain, the terror, Jim asked his friends to stop praying for his healing and restoration. Jim Hess wanted to go "Home."

"Why doesn't God take me?" he asked. 'I want Him to take me."

"It was horrible," Chere reflected. "He just wanted to go home to Jesus."

Chere now knew beyond all doubt that Jim was going to die. Calling the hospital to inform them of the change, the Oncologists suggested Jim had 2-3 weeks yet and that she should bring him in.

"I'm not bringing him in," Chere argued. "You don't know what you're talking about. I know he's not going to make it."

But they convinced her, browbeat her by Chere's estimate, into letting them send an ambulance to bring Jim to the hospital to be stabilized.

Getting settled in his room, Jim went immediately into a coma. After many hours, he unexpectedly opened his eyes, turned his head to see Chere standing by his bed and whispered through dry lips, "I love you."

Holding his hand and fighting back the flood of tears she said, "I love you too, Jim." And then they prayed together. Chere's journal entry for that day reminded her of that brief conversation with the Lord.

"So, we prayed together: 'Dear God, please take Jim home to be with you. His suffering is too great to bear.'"

Hope was gone but faith couldn't let go of the God who had never disappointed them. The one who said, "I will never leave you nor forsake you," was with them now. Hand in hand, mustering their final scraps of courage and trusting Jesus with the last throw of the dice, they walked into the Valley of the Shadow.

Forcing a thin smile, Jim Hess turned his head back to center, closed his eyes and was gone.

Four months. From the day the cancer was named until the day it took him. Four months. An eternity in 120 days.

In the fracture caused when Agape split away from the church, Chere and Jim chose to believe their Pastor and cast their lot with him. They loved Ron and sacrificed to remain loyal.

But, according to Chere, it seems he just didn't have time, ultimately blaming his schedule for what she saw as a failure of love.

Finally calling the Hess' home the Saturday before Jim died, Ron started to say,

"I heard.....," but, before he could say anything more, Chere interrupted.

"Why haven't you called? Why haven't you come to visit him? You hurt him, Ron."

Chere reported his attempt at a response.

"Well, Chere, I've been really busy and ....."

Interrupting him again, Chere's pain began to ooze out.

"That's no excuse," she responded. "You really hurt Jim by not coming."

There was no doubt that Ron was legitimately busy. In an attempt to complete three years of Bible School in 15 months, he was carrying 20 Units per semester at Fuller. Add in the demands of a growing family and congregation and it would have certainly stretched anyone in all directions.

"Well, I'm sorry about that," Chere reported Ron as saying, "God didn't lead me in that direction.

But I'd be honored to give his funeral."

Overcome by what seemed an inexcusable coldness in his response, it was more than she could bear. The only thing she could muster was, "No way. *No way.*"

"And that was my demise in the church," she sighed. "It just killed me. I left that church because of that. Never went back."

Filling in the gap for their missing Covina Park friends, Chere and Jim found comfort and spiritual healing among the good folks at the Pomona Baptist Church.

Ruth and Rolly Calkin, along with many from that congregation, had chosen to be part of Jim's "death experience," as Chere described it. In spite of what Chere interpreted as ministerial neglect, God's love found a way.

The funeral was held at Oak Park Cemetery in Montclair. "Everybody was there," Chere recalled. "It was outside, under a huge oak tree. There were hundreds of people."

This was the same Burial Ground that, three years earlier, served as the hit-and-run backdrop for the young compadres' "very cool" album cover.

Jim set up his keyboard right over there. That's where Fred stood with his back arched, pantomiming his best licks. Over there is where Mike and Richard hit their inaudible groove. A place of sweet memories and youthful fantasies, it now became Holy Ground.

186

"Ron and Eila did, graciously, come." Chere noted. "And that was nice. Ron was humble."

Looking around the seated crowd, humility was required of everyone that day. For the love of Jim Hess, all of them sublimated their own anger, resentment, sorrow and pain.

The "Storm Oil" was still exercising influence.

People do not grieve for monsters. We grieve for loveliness lost and that, sudden, vacuum pulled at every soul gathered, uniting them in an overflow of tears.

For Richard Greenburg, Mike Jungman and Fred Caban, Jim's death was the final heartbreak in many months of unprecedented sorrow. Thoughts of, "what might have been" now drove their final spikes.

Beyond broken, they were ground to dust.

There was no looking back. For any of them. Nothing they'd started could be redeemed, all of it now symbolically buried under the ancient, towering Oaks of Montclair.

"There was no time to go back to that," Chere sighed. "We were all from different places in our lives and we, kind of, went our own way."

Chere's mom referred to the Covina Park Church as, "a group of misfits that need each other." Strangely, that's what they all felt. Not for the I.A.M. part of it but for the loving family that drew all of them in the first place.

Slowly filtering out from a graveyard filled with buried hopes, embittered by religion and feeling adrift on the wind, the Azusa pilgrims set sail.

> *"It is in the deepest pain and self-doubt,*
> *in our humility and loss of ego,*
> *we discover who we really are.*
>
> *That is when we can just, Be."* [3]

---

[3] Lesa Caldarella, "Be," *Desert of this Beauty*, 2019

Jim and Chere Hess

Sharron and Mike Jungman

Lesa and Fred Caban

Still Standing

How near to heaven do you imagine Icarus ascended before learning, from "waxen-wings," that some things just don't work out? No matter how heroic or daring, no matter the purity of purpose or size of the sacrifice, sometimes, things just don't work out.

In such crucibles of grievous disappointment, it becomes easy to give up, to just fade away. The ghosts of our own failures, the absurdities of life and the disappointment of too many shattered faiths move us to become too easily sated, too easily indifferent.

Thankfully, as God continues to beckon, we exercise our will to make intelligent decisions about our feelings and stand up, wriggle into our spiritual spandex, and get going, once again.

Twenty years later, Fred Caban signed a distribution contract with *Hidden Vision Records* in Tucson, Arizona. Representing some of the earliest recordings of Jesus Rock music, business partners Richard Acevedo and John Neal took advantage of the Internet for a world-wide re-release of Agape's catalogue of songs.

Along with the music of Agape, the duo also represented the All Saved Freak Band, the Exkursions, Mike Johnson, Stonewood Cross, Selah, the Concrete Rubber Band, the Bridge and First Revelation. For many years, Richard and John, "single-handedly," kept the earliest Jesus music alive and relevant to a new generation.

Planning three reunion concerts to help promote the re-release of their music, including Teen Challenge and NAMM Jam[1], Richard and Fred set up a "CD release gig" at the Civic Plaza in Phoenix. While the original plan was for Fred to play solo, Mike and Lonnie accepted an invitation to play, expecting a rare opportunity to share Christ as they always had.

But the years, the distance and some disturbing choices from Fred – the kind best left between close friends – resulted in an uncomfortable connection between them. Expectations were left unfulfilled.

---

[1] North American Music Merchants

Following a generally disappointing event at the Civic Plaza, it was evident to all that nothing would be, could be, the same. The NAMM Jam festival, with 15,000 people in attendance, was canceled at the last-minute leaving Richard Acevedo and John Neal "high-and-dry."

It was chalked up to the cost of conscience.

"Very unfruitful, very disappointing," Mike sadly observed. "It wasn't about the future or what God is doing now. It's like we were trying to relive a past that's long gone. I made it clear to Fred that there would be no more Agape talk."

Thinking about it a little longer, Mike added, "The relationship shut down for a long time." It would be another 20 years before they embraced again.

On January 3, 2018, Fred's dad passed away. Learning of it, Mike went to the funeral to pay his respects. Because it had been so long, and there was so much "water under the bridge," Mike wasn't sure what to expect but he had to go.

A reflection of his health and his choices, the intervening years hadn't been kind to Fred. A bit surprised by his appearance, Mike offered, "Fred was looking really rough and I thought, 'Wow, Lord, am I carrying any bitterness, anger, resentment, anything? And, if so, then that needs to die.'

I can't control how he's feeling. Right? But if I'm holding *anything*, I want to air it out before we lose him. So, God was working on me and I thought, 'Well, I've got to clean this up.'"

After speaking to Fred for the first time in decades, and back home in his studio, Mike sat looking at the mementos hanging on the walls, reminiscing. Among the plaques and certificates marking his successes in life was a grainy, black and white, framed picture that Sharron had given him. An old image of an Agape performance in a park so long ago, Mike's attention was drawn to the band's logo on the drum head.

Speaking of God's incomprehensible love, it was the one, Greek word, ἀγάπη; Agape. Memories were stirred. An impulse was generated. God was still working.

"I'm looking at that logo, man, and I want something on my wall." Mike said. "I wanted it just for me and thought that'd be kind of cool."

Not cool enough to spring for a new drumhead, Mike found an old one laying around and sent it to Ernie Lewis, the artist Mike remembered doing the original.

But, when he got it back, Mike felt it lacked something of the original's "feel." As good as it was, it wasn't right. Not wanting to offend Ernie, Mike mentioned the issue to Lonnie.

"I was talking with Lonnie and somehow it came up that her daughter, Connie, is an artist. So, Lonnie volunteered her and she agreed."

In the middle of all this, Mike continued to ponder, thinking about Fred, and "How do I mend any fences?"

And then it occurred to him: "What if all three of us could sign this drumhead, *together*?"

Finally able to get a call in to Fred, Mike invited himself over to Fred's place to show him the "cool" drumhead he was going to hang in his office. But he didn't say anything about Lonnie or his intentions. In fact, he didn't know how Lonnie might feel about it. Reaching out to her again, Mike was surprised with her "being all in on it."

Lonnie added, "So we drove out, and I hadn't seen Freddie for a long time. It was a good talk. We were there for maybe 3 hours. It was just a good experience. People were still walking with the Lord." Coming from Lonnie Campbell Bissell, such an observation meant much.

Whatever the years the wounds and destructive choices may have yielded, the old friends from the Gardens of Glendora found each other in the Faith. They were *Still Standing*.

Speaking of that moment, Fred observed, "The signing of that drum head was the first time I'd seen Lonnie. I knew Mike was coming but was very surprised when I saw Lonnie. They didn't verbalize it at the time but that was a way for us to reconcile."

Reconciliation is a truly amazing possibility, especially for creatures with a capacity for offending their Creator and wounding their friends. For all the eloquent offerings of exegesis and hermeneutics, the Grace-filled act begins when one person finally decides that it's time to do the right thing.

More than an honorable truce, reconciliation is equal parts resignation and victory. Fred remembered what reconciliation *felt* like to him. "Their fellowship was like wine to me and I took it all in until I felt drunken."

Now gathered around the banner that had, for six years, promoted God's love for sinners like themselves, Fred, Mike and Lonnie made their peace. Though they might not want to hang out on weekends or be best-buds, "the middle wall of partition" between them was now broken down.

They were speaking again, spirit to spirit, mind to mind. They were able to laugh together. And they did. They were able to pray together. And they did.

God's love, ἀγάπη, never fails.

* * * *

Much has been made on these pages about calling and legacy. The two, like *Beauty and Bands*, are the bookends of all Christian service. One looks forward, the other looks back. Vision/purpose is the glue that binds them.

Fred Caban encapsulated calling and legacy. Looking back on their journey, he reflected, "Agape was our pride and joy, our calling really, and I see the music as God's word echoing in the universe; like it hasn't stopped vibrating yet. It's still bouncing around and people are still playing the music. I don't know why, but it amazes me, astonishes me really.

I believe it's because of God's word; it keeps going.

It's all very affirming, and makes me feel good, but it also tells me that I did hear God's voice and we were doing the right thing."

"I did hear God's voice," is the calling; "we did the right thing" is the legacy. "We heard and we obeyed." That's where any revival begins, where any Christian legacy finds its roots.

Agape's impact in the world is the same as that of every soul-winner, musical or not. The Sower of Matthew's parable isn't remembered for his music. He's remembered for the seed that was sown, 75% of which never bloomed. Soul-winning is about scattering joy knowing you might not reap the same.

At its best, personal evangelism is a natural, spontaneous "river of living water" that simply flows, occasionally spilling over the banks. It doesn't require a degree, a platform, a building or recognition. It only requires a humble, willing heart.

Dwight L. Moody said, "Lighthouses don't fire cannons to call attention to their shining – they just shine."

At their finest, that was Agape; that was every genre-bending pioneer, present at the birth of Christian Rock, who lifted their ax and dedicated their chops to the Lord. No pretense, no fanfare, just light.

That, and a boat-load of moxie.

Behold, a Sower went forth to sow
bearing precious seed in his hand,
hoping on Hope that he might see it grow.

Knowing that the Harvest
might well come before the bloom,
he runs on his way
there's no time to be goin' slow.

Hurry, take what you've got
and do with it what you can,
'cause the good God in Heaven
needs a Sower in the land.

Some seed fell by the wayside,
some of it fell among thorns;
some of it fell upon stoney ground.

These would never bring forth fruit
for they would not believe
that when the Sower was gone,
the Reaper would be comin' around.

Hurry, take what you've got
and do with it what you can,
'cause the good God in Heaven
needs a Sower in the land.

Lift up your eyes,
for the fields are already white.
Work while it's day, children,
can't you feel the oncoming night?

.

Lonnie, Mike and Fred

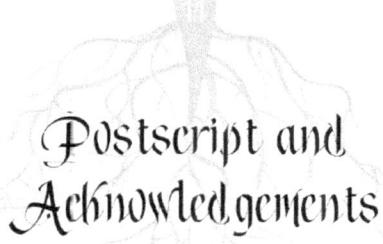

Postscript and Acknowledgements

W hen, in March of 2022, Fred Caban asked me to write the "official" story of Agape, my greatest concern was whether or not I'd be able to interview enough key people to write a credible and balanced account.

Finally able to conduct 34 interviews with 22 people over a period of twelve months, there would be no book without their combined help Words cannot express my gratitude for their trusting me with their memories.

Making sequence subject to story, several of the events depicted here actually occurred six months to a year on either side of the actual timeline. This enabled me to compress time in the narrative and stay focused on the things that mattered most. Weaving memories, I purposed to include only those reflections that began, sustained or ended the music ministry of a group of kids who called themselves, Agape.

As Woody Allen used the city of New York as both backdrop and character in several of his movies, so the Church in the Park and the Jesus Movement served the same purpose here. For me, the story was always about Agape, about what God did with Fred Caban, Mike Jungman, Lonnie Campbell, John Peckhart, Richard Greenburg and Jim Hess. My fascination was with the story of the music. What happened to it?

Leaning heavily on the participation and feedback of Pastors **Daniel Vraa** and **Jeff Newman**, I found some comfort in their ongoing-though-guarded support for the project. As cautious as they were candid, their shared adventures and perspective lent credibility to the whole.

Noticing the number of times Agape shared the stage with *Love Song*, I was able to summon the necessary audacity to contact **Chuck Girard.** Finding him as gracious in spirit as he was generous with his comments, his participation added another couple pounds of relevance and credibility to the story. Thank you for your memories.

Administrator of the *Caban Agape Archive*, **Richard Acevedo** provided many of the images used in the story and also assisted greatly in the compilation of contact information. Without Richard, it's highly unlikely I would have ever met Fred Caban. Richard's friendship and love for the earliest "Jesus music" is what brought all of us together in the first place.

When I first spoke with **Major Cornell**, he had just been released from the hospital after a year-long bout with long-term Covid. Occasionally needing to catch his breath during our interviews, his candor and matter-of-fact approach to the story helped fill in holes. Though he never got along with Ron, and left earlier than the others, his input on the beginnings of their collective journey was invaluable.

Coupling her original skepticism about the book project with her penchant for precision, **Lonnie Campbell Bissell** became one of the spiritual "sounding-boards" that helped me moderate the general tone of the story. Her details about Del and Mary Wilhite gave me confidence that I was telling their story properly.

When you want to know about a man, ask a wife. The gracious input from **Lesa Caldarella-Wong** helped me better understand some of the energies behind Fred's choices in life. Her collection of poetry, *"Desert of This Beauty,"* was written about her relationship with Fred and the Jesus Movement. I remain grateful for her generosity in allowing the inclusion of her words on these pages.

Providing the incredible details in the story of her husband, Jim, **Chere Hess** displayed the kind of courage and resolve embodied in those for whom life has revealed a cruel side. Speaking of the many nights she fell asleep while listening to Jim play his music, she wanted his story to be told. I pray her painful journey through old memories serves her well.

Speaking with a sense of lingering sadness, **Sharron Jungman** was one of several who felt the story was too easy on Ron. For her, my choice to obscure the names of the women and the minute details of Ron's reported offenses seemed to border on dishonesty.

With no attempt to diminish or minimize the reported effronteries endured by the offended, the particulars of such a story must be reserved for a different kind of book. Grateful that she was willing to speak of that defining moment in the story of Agape, I pray that time will bring peace to all the wounded memories of Covina Park.

While the accuracy of the story was important to everyone, **Richard Greenburg** was also concerned about Ron being properly honored for all the souls that were saved and all the good he'd done. "We used the music to bring people to Ron and he led them to the Lord." Focused on looking forward rather than back, it was important to Richard that honor be given to whom honor was due.

Privileged to spend more time talking with **Ron Turner** than any of the other participants, he honored me with about five hours of recorded interviews. Finding him a thoroughly likeable man, I was impressed with his willingness to discuss whatever the story demanded. He wasn't hiding from anything. The fact is, he had nothing to hide from. That's the value of repentance and forgiveness.

Perhaps a reflection of his years or his journey, Ron's memories of the band's most painful moments were different than any of theirs.

His memory of his separation from the band is that he *resigned* after returning from Lausanne. Explaining to band members that his days as an Evangelist were over, Ron felt that God had spoken to him to give his full time to being a Pastor to the Church in the Park.

When it came to Chere's memories about the passing of Jim Hess, Ron offered that he'd talked to one of the band members about visiting Jim, couldn't quite remember who, and they told Ron not to bother, that "the family didn't want him around."

With his answers raising more questions than I cared to ask, he didn't seem to recognize some of the hurtful choices he'd exercised in the lives of others. He seemed genuinely sorry to discover that some people's memories remained wounded.

In fairness to Ron, there were hundreds of people who called the Church in the Park, "home;" hundreds whose experience was more pleasurable than painful. Seeking input from the many, an internet page was launched to provide opportunity for them to participate in the story.

Providing insights for Agape's adventure, good people like **Ed Shorer**, **Richard Lopez, Sharon Newman, Steve Wilkens, Doug Haeussler and Phil Spence** of Brisbane, Australia, added much to the descriptions of the music and community that influenced their early lives. Their letters are included in the Appendix of this book.

While Fred Caban has always been spokesman for Agape, there is no doubt that **Mike Jungman** was co-founder of their ministry of music. Mike would have much preferred playing jazz or, at the least, some Kenny Loggins kind of tunes. But he believed in Fred, the music they were making and the vision they both shared.

Occasionally troubled by decisions he felt he should have made sooner, Mike continues to be a reflection of God's grace. Thank you for talking me off the ledge when I faltered.

A gentle, mirthful soul, **Fred Caban** has been a "seeker of truth" his entire, reasoning life. From *Siddhartha* by Hermann Hesse to the writings of 17th century Persian Sufis to the homeopathy of Jethro Kloss' "Back to Eden," Fred's searching made it inevitable that he would eventually run into Jesus. While Fred never abandoned seeking enlightenment, he finally found complete rest in The Truth.

When Fred asked what I thought about writing their story, I finally answered, "It sounds like a good time to me." The time spent has been good for my soul.

I remain grateful.

Appendix

Letters

Author's Page

Resources

Letters...

Sharon Newman

I joined the group (Church in the Park in Covina and Wednesday Bible Studies at APC) as a young teen through my brother, Jeffrey Newman. I am so grateful for the guidance of my brother, elder sister Sheila, Ron and Eila Turner, dear Del and Mary Wilhite, and all the loving brethren during my vulnerable youth. We grew up in turbulent times back then, potential prey to multiple social predators. The Agape family cushioned and protected one another.

Special gratitude for Lonnie Campbell, bass guitarist in Agape band, who watched over the young women in our fellowship like a mother hen. She remains a strong, intelligent, honorable and courageous role model in my heart. Her father was my college professor. Today I am a college professor. I am happy to report that Yeshua still reigns as Lord in my life. My love to all!

Phil Spence

I was introduced to Agape in 1972. I bought their first album that year. I was in my last year of high school, and discovering the music of the time, after growing up in a missionary family in Papua New Guinea.

In addition to Hendrix, Santana, and the like, I discovered Larry Norman, Randy Matthews and others. When I was introduced to Agape, I heard so many of these musical influences.

Then I began to be impacted by the lyrics that contained biblical truth. As a teenager, Agape's music was one of the influences that God used to keep me on track and pursuing the will of God for my life.

Today I lead a global network of churches and ministries, a Kingdom school with scores of locations, and have published 16 books.

Richard Lopez

Agape came out and rocked the stage. It was amazing. Then Ron Turner came out to preach and when he asked people to pray and ask Jesus into their hearts, I DID!

It was unbelievable the emotions I went through asking for forgiveness and declaring Jesus as my Lord and Savior.

After I stopped praying, I got away from the front row and took a look at all the people that showed up. There were hundreds of people; bikers, hippies, you name it. I couldn't believe how many people came out into the desert, nowhere land. The concert drifted into the next day, Easter Sunday, when Agape performed a big Baptism in the Salton Sea.

Steve Wilkens

I spent the better part of my growing up of 18 years in India as a missionary's kid. I went to countless meetings, etc. My friend, Darrell Jantz, asked me to come to Azusa Pacific College (APC) thinking I'd like it there. He'd been following the Lord for maybe a year or so. I decided that I'd give it a shot.

So, the fall of 1969 I arrived at APC. The first day he invited me to a Bible study group leader's meeting for the Agape ministry. There, I finally found some Christians I could relate to.

Till this point in my life, I always kind of believed but never really followed the Lord. That night at the group leader's meeting, it came so natural for me to just pray along with the others as they were all praying for their coming Wednesday night Bible study. At the time I did not really realize what God was doing in my life, but it was then that I really gave my life to the Lord and started serving Jesus Christ. This was my first day after arriving at APC.

All those years of going to churches, Bible studies, chapel services, our school Bible classes, etc., were going to pay off. I knew the Bible quite well, and having helped out at various Christian camps and other churches, Ron Turner asked if I'd like to be one of the Bible study leaders, and I said I would love to.

My major in college was in sports and athletics. Soon after that I changed my major to Biblical Literature. During my college years I mostly attended the Agape Church in the Park and enjoyed being one of the group Bible study leaders.

During those years when I was with the Agape ministry I went, along with many others, to help spread the gospel of Jesus Christ to many schools, parks, jails, New Year's Eve celebrations, etc., and anywhere else where people would allow us to set up the Agape Band, Heaven and Earth Band and Sunrise Band.

I remember one time we went to Palm Springs during spring break and flooded the streets, witnessing to the kids and inviting them to one of the concerts that we were going to have at the Salton Sea. Many were saved through the witnessing in the streets, and also at the concert at the Salton Sea.

It truly was the work of the Lord how God used everyone in the group to help share the gospel and see many come to know the Lord. I was with the Agape ministry from 1969 -1972.

Doug Haeussler

I was saved by the grace of God on November 7th, 1969. A high school friend, Allan Brandt, asked me if I'd like to go to a rock concert with him – so I said sure! I wish I could remember where we went for the show, but it was somewhere in the Covina/West Covina area.

A band called Heaven & Earth opened up, followed by Agape. After the show, I approached Jeff Newman from Heaven & Earth and told him I wanted to know Jesus personally too. We talked for a while and then prayed – I asked Jesus to forgive me for my sins, and I told Him that I believed He was crucified on a cross and rose again 3 days later to prove He was actually God in the flesh.

From that moment onward, I knew that Jesus loved me and had saved me from eternal damnation, just because I had decided to accept His free gift of forgiveness.

In later years, I was able to contribute to the ministry by taping each & every Sunday sermon on my little cassette tape recorder. As I recall, I operated two recorders at once, so I could get two tapes – one for Ron Turner, and the other for myself.

I also did the printing for the Agape ministry for quite a while. I ended up with a small Multi 1250 offset printing press in my garage, complete with equipment and chemical supplies.

Now, 53 years later, I realize how blessed I was to study the Word of God under Ron Turner and his wife Eila. They were probably the most loving, caring Christian couple I've ever known.

Because of Agape (the band), I flourished spiritually at Agape (the ministry). Between Wednesday night bible studies at Azusa Pacific College and Sunday morning worship in Covina Park, I was solidly grounded in the Word of God – learning to rightly divide the word of truth (2 Timothy 2:15). I'm still learning as the Holy Spirit leads!

Author's Page....

JOE MARKKO is a life-long musician and co-founder of one of America's earliest Christian Rock bands, the All Saved Freak Band. An author of six books, including his Award-Winning autobiography, "When Someday Comes: Memoirs of a Survivor," his writings are influenced by a life unusually rich in experience and tragedy.

Tempered by 10 years in a Christian cult that took the lives of three people, electrocution with 27,000 volts of electricity, the shotgun-shooting death of his oldest child, falling from grace as an ordained clergyman and the long road to physical, spiritual and emotional healing, Joe Markko's writings are intensely personal, intensely hopeful.

For more of his work visit, HomeBeforeMidnight.com

Resources ......

God's Forever Family, Larry Eskridge; Oxford University Press.

The Liturgical Renewal Movement, John W. Riggs. [Out of print]

American Jesus: How the Son of God Became a National Icon, Stephen R. Prothero; Farrar, Straus and Giroux.

Raised By Wolves: The Story of Christian Rock & Roll, John J. Thompson and Dinah K. Kotthoff; ECW Press.

Encyclopedia of Contemporary Christian Music, Mark Allen Powell; Hendrickson Publishers.

Larger Than Ourselves, Duane Pederson; The Hollywood Free Paper.

Rock 'n Roll Preacher, Chuck Girard; Worldwide Publishing Group.

Desert of This Beauty, Lesa Caldarella; Inkwell Books.

The Jesus Generation, Billy Graham; Zondervan.

www.Wikipedia.com

For more information about the earliest pioneers of Christian rock music, visit the *Jesus People Music Museum* on Facebook.

The music catalogue of Agape may be found online wherever music is downloaded or streamed.

CDs of their albums, including previously unreleased tracks, are available from www.777music.com.

www.ingramcontent.com/pod-product-compliance
Lightning Source LLC
Chambersburg PA
CBHW060918120626
46553CB00001B/365